THE LIBERAL ARTS PARADOX IN HIGHER EDUCATION
Negotiating Inclusion and Prestige

Kathryn Telling

First published in Great Britain in 2023 by

Policy Press, an imprint of
Bristol University Press
University of Bristol
1–9 Old Park Hill
Bristol
BS2 8BB
UK
t: +44 (0)117 374 6645
e: bup-info@bristol.ac.uk

Details of international sales and distribution partners are available at
policy.bristoluniversitypress.co.uk

© Bristol University Press 2023

British Library Cataloguing in Publication Data
A catalogue record for this book is available from the British Library

ISBN 978-1-4473-5947-0 hardcover
ISBN 978-1-4473-5948-7 ePub
ISBN 978-1-4473-5949-4 ePdf

The right of Kathryn Telling to be identified as author of this work has been asserted by her in accordance with the Copyright, Designs and Patents Act 1988.

All rights reserved: no part of this publication may be reproduced, stored in a retrieval system or transmitted in any form or by any means, electronic, mechanical, photocopying, recording or otherwise, without the prior permission of Bristol University Press.

Every reasonable effort has been made to obtain permission to reproduce copyrighted material. If, however, anyone knows of an oversight, please contact the publisher.

The statements and opinions contained within this publication are solely those of the author and not of the University of Bristol or Bristol University Press. The University of Bristol and Bristol University Press disclaim responsibility for any injury to persons or property resulting from any material published in this publication.

Bristol University Press and Policy Press work to counter discrimination on grounds of gender, race, disability, age and sexuality.

Cover design: Robin Hawes
Front cover image: iStock/Stas_V
Bristol University Press and Policy Press use environmentally responsible print partners.
Printed in Great Britain by CPI Group (UK) Ltd, Croydon, CR0 4YY

In memory of Neil Hough

Contents

Acknowledgements		vi
Introduction		1
1	Trailblazing traditionalists: imagining the liberal arts in time	20
2	Discipline and its discontents: multi-, inter- or trans-disciplinarity?	31
3	Distinctly indistinct: generic skills and the unique student	54
4	Jobs for the generalist: non-vocational degrees and employability	74
5	Identity and the 'ideal' student: citizens, cosmopolitans, consumers?	90
6	Meritocracy and mass higher education: character, ease and educational intimacy	110
Conclusion		134
References		145
Index		155

Acknowledgements

I am grateful to many people for their help and support over the last few years.

First, to those students and staff who gave their time to talk to me about the liberal arts.

To the endlessly patient and insightful people at Bristol University Press: Anna Richardson, Shannon Kneis, Laura Vickers-Rendall, Victoria Pittman and Caroline Astley, and to Helen Flitton at Newgen Publishing.

To the tireless transcribers of my interview tapes (and, in the latter case, my illegible hand-written manuscript): Peter Hewitt and Frankie Roake.

To those people who read a chapter and immeasurably improved the text through gentle critique: Sara Bragg, Daniel Kontowski, Aleks Lewicki, Luke Martell, Alison Phipps and Sivamohan Valluvan. Thank you for saving it from some of my worst excesses of snark and bluster; the significant snark and bluster that remain are, of course, all mine.

To the two people who read the whole thing: the anonymous reviewer for Bristol University Press and my dad, both of whom were encouraging and kind (though for different reasons).

To people who have, in different ways, helped me believe that I had something to say: Peter Watts, Tracey Potts, Peter Scott and Jeremy Lane (who is spoiling the rhyme).

In addition to the friends just mentioned, to other friends: Maddy Abbas, Clare Adams (and Jo, George and Lorna), Eva Giraud, Karis Hockey (and Joe and Ted), Helen Holmes, Kayleigh Legg, Charlotte Morris, Alexa Neale, Gemma North, Carli Rowell, Lizzie Seal, Jude Townend and Alice Wilson.

To my tolerant and, I suspect, bewildered family: my dad Chris, my mum Helen, Paul, Jim, Caroline, Cerys, Brandon and Aisling.

To Roseanne Wilding, thank you.

To Simon Speake – Telling and Speake, for keeps.

Parts of Chapter 6 and the Conclusion have been published as Telling, K. (2020) 'The complexity of educational elitism: moving beyond misrecognition', *British Journal of Sociology of Education*, 41(7): 927–41.

Introduction

Here are two tales you may have heard about what's happening in higher education in countries like England at the moment. Excuse the lack of references, but I am concerned here to give a general gloss on these accounts in their simplest forms.

The first tale concerns the marketisation of higher education. The introduction and steady (and not-so-steady) increase of tuition fees has created a volatile environment where no quantity of students is enough and no student–staff ratio is too high. Treating higher education institutions as businesses has corrupted the system, resulting in a glut of overpaid, corporate managers and ill-prepared, instrumentalist students. Box-ticking exercises have replaced a genuine concern with students' welfare, and basic research is rarely pursued due to the clamour of impact. Writing in this vein is sometimes described (though not always by the writers themselves) as 'critical university studies'.

The second tale is, among other things, a critique of this critique. While in agreement that there are serious problems in higher education today, this second story takes aim at the diagnosis supplied by the first. It claims that to focus on the ever-growing, ever-hastening university as the problem is to indulge in nostalgia for a past before mass higher education. The first diagnosis tends not to dwell for too long on remedies for the ailment, but it seems to imply that everything was better in some specific time in the past. Thus, according to the second tale, the first tale hankers after an elitist and highly selective higher education system, and is, at best, ignorant of and, at worst, indifferent to that system's history of entanglement with empire, worker exploitation, racism and sexism. Writing of this sort is sometimes described as 'abolitionist university studies'.

Both bodies of work (to which this hurried sketch does no justice whatsoever) show us important truths about higher education. Rarely does either tale claim to be the whole story. Yet, how do we account for the fact that *so many* who work or study in universities are *so critical* of both marketisation and elitism? Or, to flip over to the more cynical side of this coin, how can we account for the fact that so many of these critics (myself, for instance) continue to invest their lives in the pleasures and the pains (as well, of course, as the pay cheques) of higher education? False consciousness or simple hypocrisy? Perhaps. Or, we might be in need of a story about higher education that can account not only for marketisation and the critique of marketisation, but also for elitism and the critique of elitism (and much else besides), and that does not see hypocrisy in their entanglement. Perhaps the (piecemeal and no doubt unsuccessful) attempts of those who study and work in higher education to disentangle such knots while caught up in them have, in fact, something to teach us about education itself.

Here is a worked-through example. Many Oxbridge selectors who are mindful of the problems with admissions interviews (for instance, that they tend to favour the reproduction of the college intake as it already exists) may nonetheless wonder, on a practical level, what might replace them given that all applicants have the very highest predicted grades. In this extremely competitive situation, selectors may also be looking for qualities in individual applicants (enthusiasm, thoughtfulness, potential and so on) that seem to require some personalised method, going beyond the mere assessment of grades. Yet, it would be difficult to deny that private schools sell themselves on their ability to instil in pupils the kind of unselfconscious self-possession that goes down well in interviews of all sorts. It is also difficult to deny that such confidence may be received differently by interviewers when it emanates from a less privileged young person (see, for example, Burke and McManus, 2011). Many Oxbridge interviewers will be troubled by this and seek out unconscious bias training and the rest.

This can be described as a knot of values. Beliefs that an admissions process should be a neutral assessment of ability (what I will call 'civic values') are tangled up with ones about the importance of an individual's character (what I will call 'domestic values'). This book means to stay with the many knots of values – with the mess – that characterise higher education as it is actually experienced.

However, while it's true that we do take ideas about character into account when assessing somebody's suitability for this or that opportunity (and it may even be true that this can't, in the end, be avoided), the mere observation of this mess does not get us very far in making decisions about whether we *ought* to take character into account, or how we should do so, or how to identify when the problems have become so large that we must pause a moment and ask if we are doing the right thing.

For pause people do. In this example, and as will be seen throughout the book, people involved in education actually spend lots of time trying to disentangle the different values at play: in the case of admissions interviews, civic values stressing a neutral test of capacity from domestic ones about character. People often try, as far as they can, to be explicit about what they're testing for and what they're not, make a case to prioritise one value over another, or question the legitimacy of this or that value in a certain context. People's attempts to disentangle these messy situations need not be successful in the purist sense in order to have meaningful effects; in fact, to imagine that we have successfully solved the problems once and for all would be a mark of failure. The line between an appropriate and prudent concern with character and a discriminatory one likely to follow well-trodden lines of class, race and gender is rarely clear-cut. These are live areas for debate that people negotiate without certainty.

Therefore, in order to get a full picture of what is going on, we need to go beyond observing the knot, the mess or our inevitable complicity, to attend to questions of justice (Giraud, 2019). However, while the critical sociology of education often, following a version of Pierre Bourdieu's ideas, tries to unravel this complexity by showing that judgements about character in education are *really* ones about class (or that universities' claims to be innovative are *really* about recruiting students, or that students' concerns about their studies are *really* expressions of consumerism), I argue that this way of trying to clear the mess to see what's really going on obscures, in fact, students' and academics' sincere attempts to grapple with fairness and justice. Offering an alternative to this foundationalist way of thinking is a key aim of the book and will be expanded upon throughout this introduction.[1]

Why the liberal arts?

This is a book about the increasing number of degrees in English universities that call themselves 'liberal arts' (or something very similar). I argue that the turn to the liberal arts provides a lens through which to examine some of the plurality, knottiness and mess of contemporary higher education in stark relief.

Educational initiatives named 'liberal arts' or 'liberal education' are on the rise globally. In 2018, there were estimated to be more than 200 liberal education courses in 58 non-US countries (Godwin, 2018). England is one place that has seen significant growth, along with parts of the Arabian peninsula (Vora, 2019), China (Godwin and Pickus, 2017) and Western and Central Europe (Claus et al, 2018), among others. There are 26 higher education institutions in England advertising liberal arts degrees for a 2022 start, up from 17 five years before. They are emerging, if unevenly, right across the sector: of those 26, 11 are at old, eight at post-war, four at modern and three at private institutions.[2]

Kara Godwin (2015a) has argued that there are three broadly agreed-upon features of the liberal arts globally. First, liberal arts courses are interdisciplinary: they entail the study of more than one discipline

---

[1] For reasons of space, this book does not engage at length with Bourdieu's ideas. For previous discussion of his work and its relevance to the questions pursued here, see Telling (2016, 2020).

[2] These numbers were established using the search function of the Universities and Colleges Admissions Service (UCAS), in addition to web searches for those private institutions that do not use the UCAS service. For a full explanation of this division by age, see the following.

simultaneously. Second, they contain some notion of a broad, general education that is in some way common for all students; thus, they are not merely piecemeal dual-honours programmes, but rather take a more holistic approach. Finally, there is a focus on the development of generic skills that go beyond disciplinary training, such as communication, collaboration and lateral thinking.

Mary-Ellen Boyle (2019) notes a number of reasons that are often given for the current growth of the liberal arts, including: employers' demands for broadly educated and adaptable workers; the idea that contemporary problems like climate change require complex, interdisciplinary solutions; and the movement from elite to mass higher education systems, meaning that specialisation and vocational choices are happening later. As both Godwin and Boyle also note, however, such easy stories of a unified, global direction of travel mask a great deal of complexity. Around the world, including in England, liberal arts approaches are 'percolating not proliferating' (Godwin, 2015b: 3): they remain marginal in every national system outside North America; they do not seem to follow straightforward economic or political patterns (emerging, for instance, in both countries with a growing middle class and countries where the middle class is shrinking); and they even work counter to simultaneous global moves towards advanced *vocational* education.

Yet, there's clearly *something* going on. As one promotional website for a liberal arts degree puts it: 'Liberal Education is timely. Its emphasis on individualism and freedom of choice coincide[s] with the spirit of our time' (website, post-war).[3] Statements like this may lead more cynical observers to note a relationship between the growth of the liberal arts and a general trend towards treating students as consumers in English universities, in the context of the introduction, tripling and tripling again of home students' tuition fees since the late 1990s. The high level of optionality for students studying the liberal arts in comparison to 'traditional' degrees is a key selling point, and it would be strange indeed not to note this connection.

Yet, to focus on this aspect alone, as in some rather one-dimensional critiques of the marketisation of higher education, is to miss much of what is going on. As I show throughout the book, people involved in the liberal arts (both staff and students) bring complex and plural values to their endeavours. The notion of a competition to recruit students by giving them what they want, for instance, may help us to see something important about universities' promotional websites or what people do at open days; it is much less clear from talking to academics, and even less clear from talking to students, that competition is the best way to characterise either everyday educational

---

[3] Throughout the book, all quotations that are unattributed in this way have been taken from the websites of anonymised higher education institutions.

encounters or what people actually think they are doing in a university. As Bernard Lahire (2015) argues, sociological concepts like Bourdieu's 'field' can help us to see certain sorts of social processes, but it does not follow that every kind of context is helpfully conceived of in this competitive way.

Thus, while some people write of the *neo*liberal arts, as far as possible, I avoid the expression 'neoliberalism'. This is not because I object to the pun (I think it's quite a good one), but rather because 'neoliberalism' can become a black box, glossing over a great deal of complexity (Pettinger, 2019). The turn to the liberal arts should be understood, instead, in the context of the plural values (including but not limited to market values) that characterise higher education today.

Note, for instance, the bewildering array of meanings for the word 'liberal' in ordinary use, each of which furnishes the liberal arts approach to education with a connotation that can be more or less prominent in different settings. There are, of course, a wide range of political meanings for 'liberal', from right-wing laissez-faire economics to much more leftist ideas. It is telling that 'liberal' can be used as an insult from both the Left and the Right; indeed, in radical politics, a liberal is one of the very worst things to be. Beyond strictly political meanings, 'liberal' can mean free or free*ing*, egalitarian or elitist ('liberal intellectuals'), the ability to choose for oneself or an idea of what one *ought* to choose, education for freedom or education for those with free time, specific or general, comprehensive or selective. As Helen Small (2013: 15) notes: 'Given the splintering effects of the term "liberal", its ability to stand for quite disconnected and even contradictory ideals – wholeness and specialism; interdependence and freedom – it might well be preferable to avoid it altogether.' And yet the term is gaining currency in educational circles in England, so it must be reckoned with – not in the sense of teasing out what 'liberal' really means (which would mean discounting other connotations of the word), but rather by staying with this plurality.

As this brief introduction has already made clear, deciding on what the liberal arts are all about and why they are growing in popularity in England and globally (and, indeed, why they *aren't* growing as much as their advocates might wish) is no easy matter. An increasing number of institutions are marketing degrees named 'liberal arts' (or 'liberal education' or 'liberal studies'), true, but this does not mean that they are all marketing the same sort of thing under this banner. As the project has gone on, I have become less and less clear that I understand what the English liberal arts are.

Certainly, many of the features that are associated with the approach in the US are not present in all or even most English initiatives. (Nor are they always present in US iterations, and this is where we can really begin to tie ourselves in knots.) On the curricular level, English liberal arts degrees largely do not have distribution requirements asking that students take a breadth of subjects. Quite conversely, in the English case, students are often prevented, for reasons that will be explored in Chapter 2 on interdisciplinarity, from taking a wide range of subjects, especially in the natural and physical sciences. The major–minor structure often associated with the liberal arts in the US is also largely absent. With some notable exceptions, general education, if understood to mean something like a great books or civilisation course designed to equip all students with a broad instruction in literature, history and perhaps science, thought of as 'preparation for life', is not a feature of the English liberal arts either. Connected conceptions of holistic education, of education for citizenship or of the small, discursive class are more common but, again, far from universal.

It may be easier to specify what the English liberal arts are *not* (Kontowski, 2016) and what it is that they often define themselves against (though, irritatingly, I intend to problematise this too). In this, I depart from Kara Godwin's (2015a) helpful criteria mentioned earlier in order to distil what can be said to be true of all liberal arts degrees in the *English* case. I believe there are two features. First, English liberal arts degrees are not entirely vocational. (While some may allow students to take, for instance, engineering or accounting modules, or even to take these subjects as a pathway through the degree, there will always be a significant part of the course consisting of non-vocational subjects: history, French, chemistry and so on.) Second, liberal arts degrees depart from the traditional single-discipline model, with students taking at least two subjects – and generally more.

These are slim definitional pickings, and this may be one reason why arguments have recently been made that it is a mistake to characterise the liberal arts approach as, historically, uniquely North American at all. Philip Altbach, for instance, has helpfully brought together historical examples of non-specialist education from Confucian, Hindu, Buddhist and Muslim institutions in order to counter the narrative that the liberal arts are a distinctly 'Western' approach. His article's title is 'The many traditions of liberal arts – and their global relevance' (Altbach, 2016). But what is the logic in calling all non-specialist higher education the liberal arts? Paradoxically, to use such terminology in an effort to decentre the US is, in fact, to recentre it, as it is to use a culturally specific US term to group together highly disparate educational approaches that already have their own ways of describing what they're up to. It is only surprising that non-specialist degrees exist outside of the US if we start from a position of extreme exceptionalism.

What is of interest here is not non-specialist degrees or non-vocational degrees, which have indeed existed all kinds of everywhere for a very long time, including in England. Rather, it is endeavours that *call themselves* 'liberal' that are on the rise; thus, they are the topic of this book.

Methodological reflections: idealism, cynicism and a hierarchy of ambivalence

This book, then, is about those degrees that are being marketed as 'liberal arts', 'liberal arts and sciences', 'liberal education' or 'liberal studies' in higher education institutions (most, but not all, of which are universities) in England. In this section, I give some descriptive detail on the methods used and, especially, the approach to interviews.

The research entailed discourse analysis and interviews. I conducted initial discourse analysis of all text on applicant-facing webpages promoting liberal arts degrees at the 17 institutions offering them for a 2017 start. Some findings from this were published as a journal article (Telling, 2018). In the summer of 2017, I conducted in-person interviews with nine academics, ranging in seniority from teaching fellows to pro-vice chancellors, at three institutions in different regions of England (one old, one post-war and one modern). Two articles emerged from this part of the research (Telling, 2019, 2020). Over 2018 and 2019, I completed video interviews with 26 undergraduate liberal arts students at seven institutions (three old, two post-war, one modern and one private). While the degrees are at English institutions, they are notably international courses, and I did not make restrictions on the nationality of interviewees. Finally, I completed a new iteration of the discourse analysis, this time examining the promotional webpages of the now 23 institutions advertising liberal arts degrees for a 2019 start. All quotations from websites in the book come from this second round of discourse analysis. All names given to interviewees are pseudonyms.

One particular feature of English higher education is how prestige attaches to different institutions in connection with their age (in addition, of course, to other things). Thus, in this book, I refer to four broad categories of institution largely on the basis of their age – with an understanding that age is also an imprecise measure of prestige (as assessed, for instance, by league-table positions). The four categories of institution I will refer to and that will be used to attribute direct quotations are: old (receiving the title 'university' before the Second World War); post-war (receiving the title 'university' between 1945 and 1992); modern (receiving the title 'university' after 1992); and private (institutions, also largely modern, that do not receive government subsidies, many of which also do not have the title 'university'). This historical categorisation follows a logic, marking two points of expansion for the sector: first, post-war growth that both preceded and implemented aspects of the Macmillan government's Robbins Report (Robbins et al, 1963); and, second, growth connected to the liberalisation of access to the title 'university' instituted by the Further and Higher Education Act 1992. Nonetheless, these remain highly disparate groups, and differences of resources, selectivity and location are significant within each.

Where such institutional specificity, going beyond the broad groupings, is important, I note it.

In seeking to understand the entanglements experienced by students and staff within higher education, as well as attempts to disentangle them, I will repeatedly draw attention to a spectrum, or, more properly, a hierarchy, of ambivalence. By this, I mean to suggest that there is an increasing awareness of the plurality of higher education's complex values, as well as more sustained attempts to deal with this through disentanglement, as we travel from more privileged institutions to less privileged ones, and from individuals with more power to those with less. This is a version of standpoint theory (Smith, 1987; Harding, 1991), taking seriously the inverse relationship between power and insight.

For instance, the promotional websites of relatively elite (old and post-war) universities often portray the liberal arts simultaneously as education for social justice and as preparation of a small number of 'able' people for well-paid leadership roles. This entanglement of egalitarian and elitist values, if noted at all here, might be smoothed over with casual reference to a just society as one that has the most able individuals at its head – a rather pat meritocratic settling of any potential disquiet. The websites of modern institutions also grapple with value tensions of this sort; however, rather than seeking to settle them down, they stay with the trouble, asking explicitly what the problems are here, how universities came to serve such different interests simultaneously and even what it means to prepare someone for work at all. No less (indeed, probably more) than old and post-war institutions, modern ones must try to recruit students through their websites; however, they often do so by asking questions, not offering answers.

There is a similar hierarchy of ambivalence when it comes to interviewees. I mean to suggest that those who occupy less privileged spaces in institutions, again, tend to spend more time trying to disentangle tricky knots than those with more power. (Very) broadly, senior managers in interviews were more likely to gloss over contradictions between values, as well as less likely to note the discomfort often provoked by them, than were their juniors – and those on precarious contracts in particular. Similarly, students who received their compulsory education at English state schools or outside the English system altogether tended to stay with complexity and try to unravel these knots in order to question what the liberal arts are really doing, as well as what they could be doing, more than privately educated English students.

This example already alerts us to some of the difficulties of trying to suggest a straightforward hierarchy of this sort, for while international students are often highly insightful about the idiosyncrasies of the English higher education system, its contradictions and tensions, international *liberal arts* students are often, in fact, from relatively privileged backgrounds. There is an ambivalence to their ambivalence, then, in as much as such students tended not to reflect on class and its relationship to the liberal arts. By contrast, as will be shown in Chapter 5, English state-educated students tended to be alive to class but in ways that could gloss over the global inequalities that led international students, privileged or not, to choose English universities.

In a similarly complex fashion, parts of certain interviews were constructed between interviewer and interviewee as rather formal and distanced transmissions of information from a senior manager to a perhaps naive, young(ish) researcher. Yet, other parts of the same interview would take a distinctly conspiratorial turn, framed more equally as a conversation between lecturers – because young(ish) researchers and academic managers are lecturers too. It is in this second type of moment that ambivalence tended to come through: with their lecturer's hat on, managers could appreciate all kinds of paradoxes in their practice that the manager–researcher dynamic did not encourage to the fore.

This is because identity is always relational: it emerges in the spaces between us, and the nature of that space is liable to change. With the exception of my asking for pronouns at the beginning of interviews, any aspects of interviewees' *personal* identity (gender, class, ethnicity, national or regional identity, and so on) that are named in the book are ones that were raised by participants in the course of the interview and not the result of direct questioning. These aspects of identity come in and out of view depending on what both the interviewee and I, as participants, were trying to do in that moment.

For instance, a number of students told me that their parents had broadly National Statistics Socio-economic Classification (NS-SEC) 2, 3 or 4 jobs, such as social worker or librarian. These students had been state educated, and their parents often hadn't been to university, or perhaps they had attended later in life. Looked at 'objectively', we could create a category for these students, like 'new middle class' or simply 'lower middle class'.

To do so, however, is to reify classes as discrete categories and to miss how class as an experience is produced, negotiated and renegotiated in highly relational ways in different situations. In the context of discussing their educational histories, students in this group often stressed their privilege in relation to others, especially friends from school who had not gone on to university. 'Middle-class' was a *self*-descriptor frequently used in this context to denote privilege. By contrast, for a group of privately educated students with parents in NS-SEC 1 – jobs like doctors and psychologists, often requiring postgraduate credentials – privilege and class came up much less (if at all). Not directly asking questions about class meant that it emerged in the interview only if it was experienced as important to the participant in the specific context of their educational history.

To note this difference between interviewees is not to say that class should be *reduced* to self-understanding, and it would be absurd to say that the first group are middle-class and the second group are classless. It is, however, to suggest that whether or not somebody foregrounds class in a particular context *is itself an important aspect of class*. For students who had gone to mixed-class state schools, the privilege attached to attending university, especially to study a non-vocational course with little recognition on the job market, could not be avoided. For students with more homogeneous friendship groups, this aspect was less visible.[4] This book is, then, fundamentally interested in how class is produced, negotiated and renegotiated in specific contexts: it is about class relations, rather than *classes* (Bradley, 2014).

By taking this approach, I also do not mean to suggest that more privileged students are entirely blind to the relationship between higher education and inequality. All students I spoke to could be highly sceptical about simple narratives of higher education that are not attentive to complexity, especially around issues of injustice. Similarly, I haven't met any liberal arts student who has thoughtlessly ingested simplistic stories about the liberal arts as the inevitable direction of travel or its potential to 'rule the world' (as in Scott Hartley's [2017] rather bombastic book title). In interviews, they could be critical of their institutions, their peers and themselves, and they were often very funny with it. I hope to have captured some of this verve and, in particular, to have moved past the rather on-message student voices we sometimes read in work on the growth of the liberal arts, especially when the research itself is coming from a rather on-message place.

Yet, both students and academics simultaneously talked cynically *and idealistically* about the liberal arts – often in the same breath. They expressed sincere beliefs in the power of education to change the world, while simultaneously deriding that very idea. I hope that I treat participants' passions and enthusiasm with as much respect as their more cynical statements.

As particular sorts of social encounter, research interviews encourage certain sorts of reflection and discourage others. More precisely, the incitement to explain, and, implicit within this, to *justify*, seems to invite both idealism and cynicism; this last aspect not least because the discipline of sociology may have been understood by these discipline-savvy interviewees as a kind of professional cynicism. This does not, however, mean that idealistic *or* cynical ideas about the liberal arts are merely an artefact of the interview (Hughes et al, 2020).

---

[4] However, class *can*, of course, be reflected upon once it has been introduced. One student in this second category emailed me shortly after his interview, writing at some length about class, privilege and the liberal arts, which he had forgotten to mention. My guess is that he may have looked at my institutional profile and noted that these things were foregrounded there. This example illustrates the value in allowing issues like class to emerge over the course of the interview itself.

Luc Boltanski and Laurent Thévenot (2000) use the analogy of the rules of grammar to describe acts of explanation and justification. While native speakers do not generally talk with the rules of grammar in mind, this does not mean that if invited to explain why they had constructed a sentence in a particular way, they would simply be inventing their explanations as a kind of post hoc legitimisation. It is true that in the everyday run of things, we may not explicitly think about the rules of grammar. Similarly, we may not explicitly think about the purpose of education when sitting in, or teaching, a class. However, this does not mean that the invitation to reflect, explain and justify presented by an interview is met with mere invention out of thin air. Rather, people aim to act in ways that they will later be able to explain and justify to themselves and other people, just as people aim to speak in ways that will be intelligible to others, whether conscious of the rules of grammar or not (Boltanski and Thévenot, 2006).

As opposed, then, to an attempt to reveal the *real* reasons why someone might advocate for the liberal arts (for instance, as an expression of their class privilege), this approach tries to act with a kind of ethical credulity towards how people in interviews account for their educational experiences and beliefs. They are not masking over their real, and actually rather simple, motivations. Rather, the complexity of idealism entangled with cynicism, for example, is taken to be a sincere presentation of an *experience* of entanglement.

Cynicism can be understood as an aspect of what Andrew Sayer (2011) calls 'lay normativity', or everyday value making, just as much as idealism can. We miss how cynicism can be bound up with more hopeful feelings (Allen, 2017) when we imagine that these are two poles on a single spectrum upon which we should place individuals for all time. In fact, it may be better to think of qualities like idealism and cynicism not as opposite poles at all, so that as one becomes 'more cynical', one necessarily becomes 'less idealist', but rather as located on *separate* scales. This would suggest that they are of qualitatively different normative orders (Oldenhof et al, 2013). Thinking in this plural way about value systems may allow us to make better sense of the complex ways that people talk about what education means to them, without presenting one type of value as more sincerely felt than others. Such an approach requires us to stay with the knotty multiplicity of individuals' accounts *in speech*, which are far more complex than liberal arts advocacy in its written form.

Staying with the knot, or taking plurality seriously

Boltanski and Thévenot (2006) helpfully illustrate the existence of multiple normative orders with an anecdote about Pablo Picasso. The artist was dining in a restaurant when he was recognised by a stranger. She asked him to draw a picture on a napkin for her, insisting that she would pay whatever money he considered the napkin to be worth. When Picasso agreed, drew the picture and asked for $10,000, the woman was aghast, crying that the image had taken only a few seconds to draw. Picasso disagreed, saying that the picture had, on the contrary, taken him 40 years.

In his famous, perhaps apocryphal, response, Picasso stayed within the system of value to which the stranger had appealed when objecting that the picture had taken just a few seconds. They do not disagree that a measure of time and labour is a fair test of the object's worth, but rather on the best way to measure that worth. By contrast, Picasso *could* have sought to return the woman to other orders of value to which she had herself, after all, only recently appealed. He might have staked a claim on the basis of his intrinsic worth as an artist ('Why, this is a work of genius'), the napkin's market value ('What do you suppose this would make at auction?') or his fame ('Don't you know who I am?'). He could, of course, have decided that the dispute was not worth the ruination of a good meal and agreed to lower his price.

In this example, Boltanski and Thévenot describe a situation where Picasso has a range of options. His response is not predetermined by only one sort of claim to a shared value system that could be perceived as legitimate: his esteem as an artist; his fame (which is not quite the same thing); the market worth of his work; or the time that went into producing it. Rather, the scene is characterised by uncertainty (Boltanski, 2011). According to Boltanski and Thévenot, then, the values that people bring to bear on situations are best understood not as on a single scale, but rather as plural. These different normative orders (sometimes referred to as 'polities', and framed somewhat differently as 'conventions' in Thévenot's [2014] later work) are ways of ordering the world, based on claims made about the sacrifices made to get to a certain position and thus one's entitlement to social rewards.

This disputational context is not, of course, characteristic of all situations, but rather of ones specifically formed by conflict and appeals to justice (Boltanski, in Basaure, 2011). Before the critical moment (Boltanski and Thévenot, 1999), Picasso was simply enjoying his meal; sooner or later, he would surely go back to it. However, as I argued in my discussion of the research interview earlier, this does not mean that such value systems only appear in these moments as a post hoc form of legitimisation.

In order to describe some of the plurality explored by interviewees in this study, I make use of a number of the value systems described by Boltanski and Thévenot (2006) in *On Justification*. First, as has already been intimated, higher education remains animated by inspirational values of learning for its own sake and of creative and intellectual endeavour. People involved in universities tend to hold these values even though, as noted, they are perfectly happy to deride them too. As we have also seen, educational ideas are, at the same time, tied up with domestic values of interpersonal relationships, good character and style. While, within the critical sociology of education, we often think of such domestic concerns as an illegitimate importation of classed and other prejudices into the educational sphere (think, again, of the Oxbridge interview), progressive educators, including critical sociologists, often rely on personality and individual connection in their everyday teaching practices. This example shows some of the problems with a purist take on these issues.

A third value system to which students and academics often appeal is the civic: notions of the public good and of credentials as an impartial marker of educational worth. Here, universities have a general function for society that goes beyond (and indeed must remain unaffected by) the personal and the particular. The value of fame relates to high regard and prestige: a highly *externalised* looking around at who is held in esteem by others, regardless of the basis of that esteem. Industrial concerns relate to notions of usefulness, for instance: what skills will be most useful for the 'worker of tomorrow'? Market values in the higher education context relate to ideas about selling an 'offer' to prospective students and securing a place in league tables. They also, like industrial values, often connect to notions of employability. Here, however, these relate to how to 'stand out' on the job market; they are thus less concerned with those skills that may be required once actually *in* a job.

A key difference between the approach of this book and that briefly outlined earlier is, however, the focus on speech as where the mess of this plurality can be seen – and stayed with. For Boltanski, the written form is the place to seek and itemise different value systems. While acknowledging multiple compromises with, and critiques from, other orders, his work has sought to describe each order in turn:

> Our descriptive enterprise, conducted from within each world, requires our reader to suspend the critical outlook that results, as we shall see, from familiarity with several different worlds, and to plunge into each world in turn as one would do in a situation in which the sincerity of one's adherence to principles would be a condition of the justification of one's action. (Boltanski and Thévenot, 2006: 136)

This book takes the opposite methodological move: it seeks to stay with the mess of plurality. A key argument is that the addition of the spoken word to the written allows us to see plurality and knottiness more clearly, and that such complexity should be explored in fullness before seeking to follow one particular thread.

A familiar example of such complexity in speech is the idea of putting different hats on in order to express different points of view, all of which the speaker identifies with to some extent. We use the hat metaphor to signal a quick succession of views, in tension if not necessarily directly opposed, and where we do not wish to sacrifice any one understanding. We are foregrounding one interpretation of the situation, while simultaneously suggesting that we could also adopt another – hats, after all, are to be donned temporarily.

In my interviews with academics involved in the liberal arts, participants sometimes used different hats in order to signal that it was necessary in the modern university to go beyond what we might call inspirational values of the intrinsic worth of a certain type of education but without wishing to sacrifice these inspirational values entirely: "I mean, wearing my academic hat, I definitely see a lot of value in [interdisciplinarity] from an academic point of view. Wearing the kind of more sceptical hat, I guess, I think that it's great for employability" (Kate, teaching fellow, old); "It is a very luxurious model. ... And with my PVC hat on, in this office, that's a model that's, you know, hard to justify, hard to defend" (Alan, pro-vice chancellor, modern).[5]

It is, then, a bit of a red herring to argue against neoliberalism, marketisation or the instrumentalisation of higher education in simple fashion, as even the most hard-headed university manager, or even politician, will make reference to the social and public value of universities, and to education for individual self-flourishing, beyond economic considerations. The following is a fairly typical expression of recent Conservative governments' views on the purposes of education: 'Our universities rank among our most valuable national assets, underpinning both a strong economy and a flourishing society. Powerhouses of intellectual and social capital, they create the knowledge, capability and expertise that drive competitiveness and nurture the values that sustain our open democracy' (Department for Business, Innovation and Skills, 2016: 5).

We could, of course, see this quotation as evidence of an economic world view gobbling up other values (inspirational ones about intellect; civic ones about democracy) and using them for its own ends, so that we cannot imagine anything beyond its grasp (as in some interpretations of Boltanski and Chiapello's [2005] *New Spirit of Capitalism*). This is a conception of a common-sense neoliberalism whose wicked tendrils envelope us so fully that we cannot see beyond them: a kind of imaginative tyranny.

Yet, in speech, we see people grappling with this complexity, refusing to smooth out the tensions as if they cause no difficulties, as well as refusing to subsume one value system within one set of master values that could be said to overrule the others. The hats do not fit neatly inside each other like Russian dolls, but rather butt up against each other, coming to prominence at some points and temporarily sinking at others: a sort of hat soup, if you will.

Via the idea of staying with the mess, specifically through a focus on speech in addition to the written word, I hope the book is not a contributor to a burgeoning Boltanski industry: wholesale applications of his ideas,

---

[5] Alan refers here to his role as pro-vice chancellor, not to a shiny hat.

understood as a model for all of social life, or what Jim Conley (2015) calls the 'Saint Luc' approach. Rather, some of the value systems described by Boltanski and colleagues are, in my view, useful tools to help us see certain things that are going on when we speak about universities; where they are less useful for this purpose, they are not foregrounded.

Plurality and the liberal arts

In this spirit, each chapter takes one knotty problem for higher education today, as exemplified in talk about the liberal arts, and seeks to explore the tensions, paradoxes and plurality that animate it. In contrast to the approach that Boltanski and colleagues have tended to take (and to stretch the metaphor past readerly forbearance), the smallest unit of analysis within the book is the knot and not the thread. Each chapter follows the warp and weft of one entanglement, pursuing its argument in a spiralling rather than a linear fashion, and following different threads as they cross with others. Some may call this a neat excuse for a messy book, of course.

Chapter 1 offers some more context to the liberal arts in England by exploring the temporal knots in which it finds itself. Often appealing to the liberal arts *tradition*, both in the US and in Europe, English liberal arts degrees are simultaneously marketed as innovative. Prestige is therefore able to accrue to the liberal arts on apparently contradictory fronts, both because this is an old form of education and because it is a new one. While institutions' promotional websites quite blithely present this entanglement as positive, academics are more ambivalent, especially when it comes to the difficulties of designing a coherent degree. And while the narrative of innovation suggests agency and deliberate change, liberal arts advocates are simultaneously caught in a logic of following the crowd. There is a sense here that the liberal arts must be pursued simply because others are doing so. This infuses the thrusting narrative of institutional innovation with an underlying melancholy, especially where liberal arts degrees have not only opened, but also rapidly closed.

Chapter 2 explores competing ideas about the disciplines and interdisciplinarity. English liberal arts degrees are often presented as innovative, specifically in their interdisciplinary nature. There are, however, vastly different interpretations of this idea, from optionality or multidisciplinarity, which involves simply taking more than one subject (and sometimes only two), through the interdisciplinary idea that subjects should be in conversation with each other, to more radical, sometimes moral, beliefs that the disciplines should be surpassed altogether. It is this latter conception that institutions' promotional websites often promote. Such a simple story is challenged on the ground in a number of ways, however. First, academics draw attention to the tensions between interdisciplinary ambitions and the structures of English higher education, including considerations of modularisation, specialisation and progression. Second, students interrogate some of the limitations of one of the key features of interdisciplinarity as they experience it: the application of knowledge to specific problems from the 'real world'. Paradoxically, this application entails a narrowing down of educational interests (poverty rather than politics; climate change rather than chemistry) in ways that work directly against a key tenet of the liberal arts: *general* education.

With this in mind, Chapter 3 explores a very messy educational knot that can be summarised as the tension between the general and the particular. As we have just noted, a key characteristic of the liberal arts approach is its connection to general education. While general education can be understood in different ways, one of the relevant meanings here is the idea of becoming a generalist, rather than a specialist. This chapter problematises that distinction by showing that students often think about specialisation as something that should come later in their educational career than at the end of school, rather than as something that they reject in general. This points to a further complication of the liberal arts narrative. As more students enter higher education, it is perhaps logical that a desire for general education should move up the system (leaving specialisation to postgraduate work, itself now accessed by more and more of the population). However, simultaneously, this move towards a mass university system leads to a desire from students that their credentials should help them *stand out* in the crowded graduate job market. Thus, the liberal arts simultaneously seek to satisfy student desires for generalism and particularity.

Chapter 4 builds on this idea of standing out on the job market by examining in more detail how liberal arts advocates talk about employability and, crucially, how students develop different strategies to manage what the future of work may bring. Institutions' promotional websites often simultaneously offer a picture of work that is highly concrete ('the real world') and extremely nebulous ('the unknown future'). Students sometimes question such narratives, however: first, by seeking to bring a different real world to the fore – one that challenges the idea that education is merely workplace preparation; and, second, by developing strategies to manage the unknown future that do not necessarily align with those that institutions' websites encourage. This is especially true for those students without a financial safety net.

Chapter 5 explores aspects of student identity. Good citizenship and cosmopolitanism are held in high esteem within liberal arts advocacy, not just as what non-vocational education will produce, but as what makes for a good applicant in the first place. I argue that both types of ideal identity are in complex entanglement with social class – as a number of students observe. The second half of the chapter explores the vexed issue of student consumerism. While institutions' websites stress that the liberal arts are well suited to today's students due to their bespoke (and thus individualist) nature, and some senior academics with relatively little recent contact with students argue that fees have made students increasingly instrumentalist, more junior staff, along with students themselves, had rather different things to say.

These are knotty problems, then, and the purpose of each chapter is precisely not to disentangle them once and for all in order to find one thread that is the fundamental truth of the situation. One objection that might fairly be made against such an approach is, however, that it depoliticises the sociology of education, merely describing complexity, rather than seeking to diagnose problems or come to a judgement, much less propose solutions. While the attempt to foreground the incisiveness and cynicism of students is, I think, a sort of critique in itself, it is in Chapter 6 that the question of justice, specifically in relation to ideas about character and their relationship to meritocracy and elitism, is pressed. This is precisely not, though, in order to unveil that highly classed notions of character or flair are the *truth* of what the liberal arts are all about.

In both Chapter 6 and the Conclusion of the book, the question is asked: what are the liberal arts testing for? And in what sort of educational setting is such a test appropriate? The enmeshment of domestic criteria (character, interpersonal relations, the perception of ease and well-roundedness) with others may be unavoidable, but this is not at all the same as allowing them free reign. I argue finally that the turn to the liberal arts entails a specific and often quite concerted testing for domestic values within the educational sphere, going beyond the inevitability of entanglement. This is a problem notwithstanding the fact that some students express ambivalence and insight about these elitist tendencies.

Conclusion: for unhappy hairdressers

A few years ago, there was a story in the news about a woman who owned a hairdressing shop. She had placed an advert for a new employee on the Job Centre website but been told that she must take it down because she had requested that applicants be 'happy'. She was told that this discriminated against the unhappy (Lumley, 2020).

In a drunken conversation that quickly descended into absurdity, my partner and I debated the merits of this case. His immediate sympathies fell with the woman who owned the hairdresser's shop, and who simply preferred not to hire someone with whom she would not want to go for a drink after work. In characteristically contrarian style, my sympathies fell with the Job Centre jobsworth. One should not, I thought, make decisions about who deserves this or that professional opportunity on the basis of personal criteria like happiness or niceness. In the end, my argument became that there should not be cover letters or job interviews or references at all, but rather some fully depersonalised and anonymous selection system, perhaps involving algorithms and robots.

There is, of course, a fundamental silliness to the po-faced purity of my approach. As Andrew Sayer (2020: 461) notes in his exploration of the different uses to which a concern with personal character can be put, recruitment is an instance where it would be absurd *not* to look for a colleague who was 'conscientious, honest, collegial, respectful to others, non-sexist, and so on'. Character, while hardly the only thing one needs to think about here, is not irrelevant either. In Boltanski and Thévenot's (2006) terms, we could say that I lack prudence, or an acceptance of complexity; in lay terms, I am a prig. In practice, high-minded ethical ideals can be indistinguishable from a lack of common sense.

I maintain, nonetheless, that our Job Centre friend was right to question the appropriateness of the happiness criterion to the recruitment process – just as the Oxbridge selector is right to question the appropriateness of the charisma criterion to the admissions interview. In their acts of dissent, what they are refusing is an understanding of the matter as settled – or, worse, an understanding that because we cannot get to perfection, we should not try to get anywhere better than here.

In the example of the happy hairdresser, happiness is required as a general facet of personality that endures across spheres. It is not situation dependent. Anyone can be happy in the pub or on their birthday or when fussing a big dog; the obligation here is to be happy *despite being at work*. Such a claim on the soul is fairly called tyranny.

In a similar vein, by stressing that general education is the best sort of education for every context (employment and politics and travel and social life and 'life' in general), liberal arts advocacy often oversteps what should reasonably be claimed for an educational endeavour if it is to avoid elitism. The increasing entanglement of domestic values within the liberal arts is a problem because it allows multiple goods to stick together in the person of the generally educated graduate, who deserves not just a certain type of job, but a fulfilling life, and to be recognised not just as someone with a degree, but as someone who is cosmopolitan and well-rounded – well-*respected* (yes, better respected than others). A liberal arts education is thought to lead not just to the best sort of job, but to the best sort of *life*.

The argument in the end is certainly not that the non-vocational disciplines (and the humanities in particular, which often take a symbolic place at the heart of English liberal arts degrees) are less valuable than vocational or specialist educational endeavours. In a policy context in which the arts and humanities are often relegated in favour of those subjects that apparently have more real-world relevance, stating a clear case for the importance of these subjects is vital. Yet, when it claims (however implicitly) that this type of education is not merely one option among others, but rather the best sort of education, involving the best sort of people, liberal arts advocacy in fact maintains the elitism associated with these disciplines, for to say that this education is the best, and that it is *for* the best, is always silently to exclude the rest.

1

Trailblazing traditionalists: imagining the liberal arts in time

This chapter offers some further context on the liberal arts in England and, in particular, foregrounds how senior academics describe their efforts to get a liberal arts degree on the books (and, in some cases, *off* the books). The broader context of English higher education's marketisation is important here: clearly, with a national funding model where the money follows the student, curricular innovators must make a business case to their institutions. This will generally hang on the twin hooks of student recruitment and cost effectiveness. These academic-to-institution justifications are important, including to those academics doing the justifying, and are generally not experienced as only hoops through which one must jump. The responsibility to recruit and to contribute to a sustainable institution is taken seriously by academics.

Yet, it is clear that this is not all that's going on. Mantras of either efficiency or giving students what they want do not account for the fact that at many institutions, student recruitment is not actually expected to be particularly high (though *poor* student recruitment is certainly the main reason given for the closure of liberal arts degrees). At some institutions, relatively small student intakes are positively desired (though this remains in tension with the need to recruit), and both the introduction of new core modules for small cohorts and the increased need for academic advising are hardly efficiencies. Instead, we should think about market concerns as entangled with a plurality of further values, including: a conservative domestic register of trust in the past; ideas about fame, repute and likeness with competitors; and an inspirational mode that prizes innovation and change. A complete picture of higher education today must contend with all this.

Therefore, just as the market for students should not be understood as the fundamental truth of the liberal arts, nor should we treat the proclaimed innovation of these degrees as a mere cover for elitism. It would be easy, for instance, to understand the turn to the liberal arts in English higher education as a mere re-traditionalising impulse: a longing look backward to some gilded past before application, vocationalism or even disciplinary specialisation contaminated the hallowed halls of higher education. The aristocratic undertones of liberal arts advocacy are a central concern of this book and should not be discounted as coincidental. Nonetheless, to stop at this observation is to simplify a much knottier picture. The fact that those who promote the liberal arts often point to the past in various ways does not negate the fact that these are highly innovative degrees in the English context and that they certainly do not merely replicate any particular version of the US liberal arts idea. In fact, rather like the often revisited refrain of 'modern apprenticeships', liberal arts degrees invoke a reassuring past as well as a thrusting looking forward, a combination so bold that it is presented as able to fix such inconveniences as the actually existing labour market (Ainley, 2016a). As this chapter will show, liberal arts degrees become connected not just to an approvingly invoked past, but also to some irresistible future.

In the spirit of staying with this complexity, this chapter does not offer a history of the liberal arts as such. (Good places to start for such a history include Kimball [1986], Oakley [1992] and, for the English context, Rothblatt [1976].) Rather, my interest is in how the history of the liberal arts gets told, and put to work, by institutions and individuals justifying their value in the present. It is, as in Clare Hemmings's (2005: 118) useful definition of historiography, a 'concern … with the contested politics of the present over the "truth of the past"'.

The chapter begins with an exploration of the entanglement of heritage and innovation. When it comes to the websites of elite universities, there is a compact of oldness and newness. Tradition is used to evoke a safe pair of hands; yet, tradition without innovation also suggests complacency. However, both the websites of less prestigious universities and less 'traditional' students in interviews (such as those from overseas) seek to disentangle some of this complexity by asking questions about what the important values really ought to be here.

With reference to these complex ideas about innovation, the chapter next addresses itself to the claim that liberal arts degrees are somehow the inevitable 'direction of travel' for higher education. This perception became clear in how some senior managers who were very involved in introducing the courses at the administrative level talked in interviews. There is an inevitability to liberal arts innovations because the liberal arts are a growing trend nationally. As Tim, a dean of faculty who had been involved in introducing the degree at a post-war institution, put it, it was a "no-brainer", and here comparison was especially made to very elite institutions that had seen quick success. On the other hand, for academics more involved in developing the detail of what such a degree looks like in practice, looking around at what other English institutions are doing in fact produces more questions than answers, as degrees named 'liberal arts' often look little like each other at the modular and structural level.

The difficulties of creating and sustaining a liberal arts degree are explored further in the next section, which looks at what I call 'the other direction of travel'. Here, the fact that a number of liberal arts degrees have in fact been taken off the books after only a very few years, often due to poor student recruitment, is connected to academic acceleration (Vostal, 2016), or the feeling that higher education does, and must, innovate at a heightened rate. While this other direction of travel was presented with much the same bullish pragmatism by managers as the first one, I argue that the feeling of the future as inevitable *irrespective of which future should come* means that there is a distinct melancholy entangled with the language of innovation.

Overall, I argue that academics involved in designing and sustaining (and closing) liberal arts degrees 'externalise' (Luhmann, 2002), or look around for, inspiration, both within and without the English context, settling on liberal arts degrees as one possibility for establishing meaning and a clear direction of travel when the purpose of higher education feels difficult to get purchase on. By weaving between different types of justifications, liberal arts websites seek to produce meaning for their endeavour – meaning that, I will argue, proves elusive. Rather than following some inevitable 'direction of travel', as is sometimes claimed, I argue that the peculiar rise (and, in places, fall) of the English liberal arts can better be understood as a process of institutional managers grappling for meaning where they don't really know what higher education is up to, or for. Calls for more vocational higher education appear just as often as ones for general education, sometimes at the same institution and in response to the same economic conditions. However, both relatively junior academics trying to design degrees more practically and some students concerned with the risk that they are taking on a new degree attempt to disentangle this mess.

Something old, something new: the knot of prestige and innovation

> To be an innovator, one must understand the past in its best context to identify the needs of the future and develop the innovations to anticipate and meet them. (Student testimonial, website, post-war)

This heading comes from one relatively elite institution's webpage on 'reasons to choose the [liberal arts] degree' and conveys well the weaving between tradition and innovation (sometimes in the same breath) that characterises old and post-war liberal arts degrees' promotional attempts. This is both in relation to the (prestigious, yet innovative) institution in general and to the liberal arts specifically as an endeavour at once pedigreed and progressive. In this section, I argue that this entanglement of the orders of prestige and inspiration serves to ward against accusations of both old-fashionedness and upstartery in the same breath. It is the promotional websites of modern universities, however, that seek to ask more complex questions of the history of the liberal arts, and it is international students, outsiders to the intricacies of English institutional hierarchies, that are clear about the market worth of a prestigious university's name. And it is being in a less privileged position in relation to others that facilitates both types of insights.

The website of one old institution notes that its degree draws on 'our university's exciting heritage', a strange juxtaposition that reminds potential applicants of the safe hands they are in even while seeking to suggest newness. This connection to tradition, especially at more elite institutions, foregrounds the prestige that remains central to their offer (Brewer et al, 2002) and mitigates the possible risks associated with curricular innovations. One post-war institution's website alludes casually but reassuringly to the fact that while innovative, liberal arts degrees are nonetheless cropping up in all the right places: 'While many individual institutions have long incorporated aspects of the liberal education approach, recently a number of leading Russell Group (research-intensive) universities have set up liberal education degree programmes.'

Tradition is central, then, but so too is newness. This is partially because merely appealing to pre-established prestige is an increasingly distrusted approach in many walks of life (Boltanski, in Basaure, 2011). To suggest that one is in a safe pair of hands simply because of an illustrious history leaves institutions open to accusations of complacency. Liberal arts may have such a history, but this history must be rethought for contemporary times, as this post-war institution's website puts it: 'At [this university], we've reimagined what a Liberal Arts education means for the 21st century, driven by the core values of critical thinking and the acquisition of adaptable expertise.'

Unambiguously approving allusions to the past are off-limits for institutions in relation to the liberal arts, in particular because of the more problematic aspects of the history of that tradition, specifically the use of 'liberal' to mean 'free', invoking quite explicitly the exclusion of slaves in the Roman *artes liberales* from which the modern term is derived. For Larry, who had been heavily involved with setting up a liberal arts degree at his elite, old university as a dean of faculty, it was important to stress that the link between slavery and the liberal arts was firmly and unambiguously in the past: "The ideal of freedom became metaphorical rather than literal, you know. It was literal in ancient Rome but metaphorical now. You know, freedom – knowledge sets you free from the trammels of ignorance, you know."

Less elite, teaching-focused institutions are also concerned with this link. Their widening participation remit, in particular, sits uneasily with the exclusionary history of liberal arts provision. One modern university, for example, uses the term 'modern liberal arts' on its website to distinguish itself from that older tradition quite explicitly: 'It used to be an education available only to an elite within society, but this is no longer the case. At [this university] Liberal Arts can be enjoyed by everyone.' However, rather than relegate this history to the past, the modern university's website also acknowledges the existence of *modern* slavery and the complex entanglements of universities with inequality in the present. The tangle is not glided over, and the question is not considered settled.

While elite universities entangle inspiration and prestige together closely on their websites, some of their students were clear that prestige came out on top. For international students (keen observers of, but relative outsiders to, the complex hierarchies of prestige among English institutions), only a university of international renown could make taking the risk of having a strange degree on one's transcript conceivable. As second-year student Mathilde, originally from France, explained: "And there is also the [university] label that makes it safe. I wouldn't have done that in another uni, I think, or not – I wouldn't have done it in a not-prestigious uni. Because I would have thought that it wasn't safe enough." Quite explicitly, it was prestige that meant Mathilde could consider this degree to be safe.

On their promotional websites, then, elite institutions entangle a radical and inspired image with the reassuring weight of tradition. This compromise allows prestige to remain central, while complacency and stuffiness are apparently eschewed. On the other hand, for those students concerned with the market value of their degree (especially when few English institutions carry any market heft in their home countries at all), there is real clarity that prestige trumps much else. Meanwhile, the promotional websites of less prestigious universities, rather than blithely settling the question of the liberal arts' more problematic history, continue to ask questions about the specific values that underpin the tradition. In both cases, it is a degree of outsidership that leads to some insight about the entanglement.

The direction of travel: following, leading and the logic of the liberal arts

This heading of 'the direction of travel' comes from an anecdote told to me by a friend. They had been in a meeting where their institution's new liberal arts degree was being discussed. Questioned on why such a degree was being mooted now, they were informed with some sagacity by a senior manager that this was "the direction of travel". As the story was told to me, this phrase forestalled the possibility of further questioning on the *why* front and even suggested that *why* was not the relevant question. Somehow, it is obvious that this is what we should be doing: there is an inexorable movement in this direction, which we must join or become 'of the past'. We are doing it because they are doing it. However, in this section, I argue that while the direction-of-travel argument is a key feature of how managers with *administrative* responsibility for getting liberal arts degrees on the books talk about them, for those closer to the ground and trying to plan the degrees out at a practical level, the fact that liberal arts degrees are everywhere throws up more questions than it solves.

Liberal arts degrees were formulated as the inevitable direction of travel at all three universities at which I talked to academics. However, status hierarchies were important in the different ways this was conceived. At both the old and the post-war institutions (and, to an extent, at the modern one too), academics made comparisons to elite universities with little acknowledgement that liberal arts degrees are emerging across the sector.[1] Sometimes, this concentration on elite competitors had led to unrealistic expectations about the magical effects a liberal arts degree might have on student recruitment for struggling departments. For instance, post-war dean Tim described his inspiration for the degree as partly sparked by one very elite institution that would frankly recruit well whatever they were peddling: "They'd aimed at 50 and ended up with 90. And then, when I next talked to [the programme director], he said, 'Well, it's obviously a winner isn't it? So, we pushed it up to over a hundred.'" This focus on what others are doing leaves to the side whether that is the right path to pursue in one's own institutional context.

Those at older institutions, on the other hand, might regard their *own* university as central and innovative on the higher education landscape. Rather than looking around at what others are doing, it was stressed that *this* institution is a leader, not a follower. Maria, the programme director for the liberal arts at an old university, thought that "We weren't really following other people. We sort of felt that we were at the forefront."

Yet, for Larry, a dean at the same institution, one factor was that the new vice chancellor was "looking for ways to catch rising trends." The most senior people at this elite institution, at least, were apparently looking around to others for ideas. The inspirational mode, with its indifference to what others may be up to, is here tempered by the realism of how one's innovation fits into a broader landscape. A compromise is reached between these values of inspiration and prestige, so that the institution becomes neither follower nor leader, but rather a kind of bellwether for change, as Maria explained: "But what became really obvious was that this was something that was kind of really in the air."

However, while relatively senior university managers may note that liberal arts degrees are everywhere, and thus that producing one for one's own institution is a no-brainer, for those seeking to put the idea into practice, the liberal arts are most definitely a brainer. This was illustrated to me by the humorously recounted travails experienced by Adrian, who had designed the

---

[1] The tendency for institutions of all stripes to be most aware of elite universities and, in turn, for those more prestigious universities to consider themselves to be the sector is played out in various ways, for example, in the elite Russell Group's inclination to put out press releases on everyone else's behalf.

liberal arts degree at his post-war university largely single-handedly while a senior lecturer. Here, he discusses conversations about levels of optionality within the degree and demonstrates how unclear and knotty the apparent 'direction of travel' is in practice:

> 'So, we went from that kind of very much "spine and then freedom" into "a spine and then areas of concentration", which went backwards and forwards. And we had vaguely theoretical conversations about, "What's an art?" and, "What's a science?" And so, I went – initially said, "Well okay, you have a major area and then you have a minor area, which has to be on a different theme." So, we started off by saying, "Okay, there's arts and there's sciences." And then we were thinking and looking at the marketing and what other people were doing. Then, it was self-evident that a lot of people aren't really interested in doing sciences; they're interested in doing, you know, social sciences. So, we ended up with "Arts, Social Sciences and Sciences". And then Engineering weren't happy that it was called "Sciences", so there was a lot of getting hung up on names. Endless!'

In fact, the sheer variety of approaches in England mirrors quite well the very complex history, and indeed the current picture, of the liberal arts in the US. Deciding that you are going to design a liberal arts degree is the least of the challenges. Is the inspiration a liberal arts college, with its small classes and residential character (a model that has gained more currency in parts of mainland Europe than in England), or rather a liberal arts *degree*, perhaps with some notion of a broad general education leading into final specialisation in the form of a major? Should it function as a flagship initiative for the 'best' students, as in the growth of honours programmes in the US, part of the complex ecosystem of the research multiversity? Should there be pathways or themes, prerequisites or distribution requirements, a common core, a great books programme, or the free play of electives? Merely deciding, as a senior manager, that something called a 'liberal arts degree' is the way to go does not help more junior staff much in terms of either the practicalities or the philosophy of the degree.

Perhaps to move past some of these difficulties and create a narrower meaning, on promotional websites, attention is sometimes drawn to the European tradition of liberal education, as opposed, or at least in addition, to that of the US. However, as you might gather from this switch to the language of liberal *education*, in order to make the appeal to a European tradition stick, the concept must in fact be broadened out even further than its already-expansive US understanding. Here, appeals might be made, explicitly or implicitly, to a vast array of really quite diverse precedents, including among them the ancient world's *artes liberales* or education for free men,

Italian Renaissance humanism, 19th-century German *bildung* or learning as self-development, and Oxbridge collegiate culture: 'This core programme of thinking critically across disciplines has been used to train free thinkers, visionary leaders, and intellectual revolutionaries for thousands of years. It has been continually reinvented and reimagined in every historical period from antiquity to present day' (website, post-war). This attempt to stretch the concept both geographically and historically can be so extensive that the term really just comes to mean 'education in more than one subject'.

Perhaps the more-or-less frantic looking around at what other institutions are doing speaks not of a clear direction of travel at all, but of a radical rudderlessness. There is no clear answer to the diverse and complex questions asked of contemporary higher education, and there are just as many responses to modern economic conditions that call for more vocational training, as witness the perennial resurrection of apprenticeships. Indeed, channelling Douglas Adams, we might wonder how we can get to any clear answer when we do not know what the question is. Having looked around for options, we *may* seize upon (a particular conception of) the liberal arts, but the solution only throws up further questions: 'instead of reducing the excess of possibilities, by highlighting the right decision to take, more knowledge makes even more visible the fact that other ways of doing are possible, thus stressing even further the contingency of all choices' (Mangez and Vanden Broeck, 2020: 682).

The pace of change, or the *other* direction of travel

Living in a state of change is the new normal. (Website, private)

Despite the fact that liberal arts degrees are the seemingly inevitable direction of travel, two of the three institutions at which I interviewed academics were actually in the process of discontinuing the degrees. For senior managers, this rapid closure was *also* somehow the inevitable direction of travel: analysis of student numbers over a very short time frame (as little as two years) could somehow tell an unambiguous story that the endeavour had been folly. As Alan, a dean at a modern university in the process of closing its degree, told me: "I think every trend in UK education at the moment is against the true philosophy of liberal arts." This was despite a simultaneous narrative that was quite indistinguishable from that told by other academics: that more and more students want this kind of education; that all universities should be moving in this direction; and that higher education goes wrong when it offers excessive disciplinary specialisation given current economic conditions.

In this section, I argue that the inspirational mode, with its agentic manager at the centre – thrusting ahead and making changes all over – is actually deeply entangled with a strong sense of inevitability. This takes the form of a hard-headed pragmatism about market considerations (that is, student recruitment). However, since they can seemingly conceive of any particular future as inevitable (lots of students or barely any), managers actually lose their capacity to present themselves convincingly as agents *creating* the specific future that will come.

To be worthy in the world of inspiration, innovation and genius, one must always be ready to shake off 'the shackles of habit' (Boltanski and Thévenot, 2006: 237), and nothing should be off-limits or beyond critique. As Adrian, the lecturer who, as we have seen, had largely designed the liberal arts degree at his post-war university, noted in relation to the general culture at his institution:

> 'I think one of the things that's interesting is that people still have an awareness that the job should never be done, that we should always keep on looking at what we're doing. So, I think there is much more awareness that you can't rest on laurels. And I've seen very successful bits of the university that, even though they've got very good evaluations of their teaching and good NSS [National Student Survey] figures, are still kind of reinventing what they do to make sure they keep on at the front, you know.'

Such a relentless moving forward is felt by many who work in universities, as the burgeoning 'slow scholarship' movement makes clear (Great Lakes Feminist Geography Collective, 2015; Berg and Seeber, 2017). Both liberal arts promotional websites and many interviewees stressed that flux and acceleration characterise contemporary life.

This inspirational mode was strong among senior managers I talked to, combined with a hard-headed, businesslike approach suggesting that the only response to an apparently low-recruiting degree is its immediate discontinuation. The narrative is one of tough decisions, balance sheets and the bottom line. As Tim, a dean at Adrian's post-war institution and a strong advocate of the liberal arts on intellectual grounds, noted: "I mean, the numbers were too low to – as I said earlier on – really, they're too low in terms of certainly the money we're getting. Compared with the money that you could be getting if you translated those numbers – put them back into something like English." This despite the fact that the degrees had barely bedded in, and the shortfall in student numbers was often slight too.

While they clearly pull in opposite directions, both 'direction of travel' narratives (the one that advocates for, and the one that advocates against, the liberal arts) suggest that the pace of change remains fully external to any individual will, even of deans of faculty. The institution itself is here experienced as a kind of ghost ship, buffeted by external forces without trajectory, captain or rudder ('Liberal arts degrees are the direction of travel: let's do one'; 'We didn't get enough students this year: let's knock it on the head'). In interviews, managers' bullish pragmatism was sometimes difficult to distinguish from a deep nihilistic sadness. Such defeatism relates to reality's excessive *felt realness*, which makes alternative paths seem impossible (Boltanski, 2011).

I felt such an atmosphere of defeat keenly during time spent on the post-war university campus. Yet, this was also the university where participants most discussed the proactive and forward-looking character of the institution; as lecturer Adrian, again, noted: "a lot of, you know, doing stuff, and being thrusting". Thrustingness is the other side of the coin of defeatism, which is a particular feature of those institutions, often post-war in the English context, who find themselves in the middle of status hierarchies for both teaching and research (Telling, 2019). Ansgar Allen (2014) tells a story about a colleague who could argue until blue in the face for Oxbridge interview preparation in comprehensive schools, despite knowing that this barely touched the sides of structural educational inequality. He knew that it might even reproduce inequality via its valorisation of social mobility for a tiny number as some kind of solution to structural problems. Faced with the retort that this was a mere rearranging of the deckchairs, he replied: 'You are right ... *but I just can't allow it*' (Allen, 2014: 4, emphasis in original). Opening and closing degrees is one way of doing *something*, rather than nothing, in a situation where you may otherwise be overwhelmed by a lack of control.

While academics at all three institutions commented on their experiences of a perceived speeding up of academic life, we should, then, remain mindful of the ways in which position in status hierarchies affects this experience, as well as autonomy in dealing with it. At the old university, academics and managers had taken a leisurely trip to the US when planning their liberal arts degrees, and were, as programme director Maria put it, "wined and dined". At this university, the degree also took a long time to get on the books due to the apparently glacial nature of the relevant committees – and it is still going. By contrast, the desire for a rapid rate of change, related to the industrial concern with efficiency, is particularly notable in the post-war university context and likely to be at odds with leisurely ideas about education that can be maintained in more elite university spaces.

Conclusion

The expansiveness of the meanings of liberal arts in the US context (never mind if we start including every type of non-vocational education from every time and place) means that while the term is latched on to *as if* it creates stability and meaning, it does not seem to answer any particular question – or identify what the relevant questions are. It is a black box to which may be added any number of really quite different ingredients (to mix metaphors grossly), and while this no doubt contributes to its appeal for senior managers on one level, the decision to create a liberal arts degree throws up more questions than it answers for academics writing degrees on the ground.

This chapter has drawn out some key differences between institutions of different statuses and their relationships to the temporalities of the liberal arts. It has also focused on the words of senior managers, at times, contrasting these with those of more junior colleagues at the coalface of making the degrees work in practice. Thus, it has sought to draw out power differences and how these affect conceptions of change and tradition. Due to its focus on degree design and workplace hierarchies, it has tended not to engage too much with the voices of students. By contrast, the rest of the book foregrounds students' insights about the nature of their degrees and, in particular, their attempts to disentangle some of the knots that higher education finds itself in. This begins in Chapter 2, where we turn to what may be the only feature that unites all English liberal arts degrees: their interdisciplinarity.

2

Discipline and its discontents: multi-, inter- or trans-disciplinarity?

> Put them all together, and you'll be ready to disrupt boundaries and embrace complexity. As an innovative leader of the future, with an advanced understanding of how the past impacts the present, you'll be ready to design solutions to society's toughest problems. (Website, post-war)

Like the subtitle of Scott Hartley's (2017) recent book, *The Fuzzy and the Techie: Why the Liberal Arts Will Rule the Digital World*, the quotation in this chapter's epigraph encapsulates some of the promises that are made for a liberal arts education at the more hyperbolic end. In some quarters, the liberal arts are taken to be the key to solving all manner of apparently wicked problems, from rising sea levels to knife crime. In particular, the 'real-world' character of such degrees is often connected to their interdisciplinary nature: the approach is able to solve problems in the real world because it is not held back by the artificial divisions (and therefore restrictions) of the disciplines.

In this chapter, I argue that a tendency towards *hyper*-interdisciplinarity (Moore, 2011) contributes to this sense of the liberal arts as the solution to the future's problems. Hyper-interdisciplinarity is the belief that disciplines create problematic siloes for knowledge and must be broken down in order to facilitate access to the world as it really is. Such hyper-interdisciplinarity takes for granted the idea that disciplines are regressive because they take us away from 'real' knowledge, which is thought to be situated unproblematically in the 'real' world. Here, looking at specific, concrete problems in an interdisciplinary way is thought to give access to this real world and, in turn, to bypass the fustiness and unreality of the old-fashioned disciplines.

In this chapter, I show that, as opposed to this hyper-interdisciplinary register coming from both promotional websites and some senior managers, students, in different ways and often very subtly, launched critique. They questioned the idea that disciplines are inherently progressive or regressive, offering a less positivist and more pragmatic account of the real world and its relationship to disciplines. Certainly, as we will see, some students expressed hyper-interdisciplinary ideas, but they tended to do so less often and less simplistically.

Interdisciplinarity is one of the only agreed-upon features of the English liberal arts. Yet, even here, there are multiple, sometimes competing, values at play. Indeed, these are not just problems for the liberal arts, but ones that touch upon a broader set of concerns for higher education today.

On the one hand, universities feel pressure to give students what they want, and early iterations of the English liberal arts often presented themselves on promotional websites as 'pick and mix' degrees in just this vein. This is a conception of interdisciplinarity in which anything goes: education as consumer choice. Yet, such market values are strongly tempered by concerns for rigour coming from both academics and students. Industrial ideas about hard work and progression from one stage to the next are used as critiques of pure consumerism, not just by academics, but by students too.

The chapter first discusses the problem with disciplines themselves, as conceptualised on websites and by senior academics and some students. The answer to these problems with the disciplines is sometimes given as multidisciplinarity (that is, students studying more subjects than the traditional single-subject degree still favoured in England); however, more often, it is formulated as *inter*disciplinarity, or as different disciplines actually speaking to one another rather than merely coexisting in a particular student's curriculum. In practice, however, there are multiple barriers to dialogue between the disciplines happening in this way, and the chapter goes on to address itself to these; in particular, how ideas about specialisation and progression in England, not just in higher education, but at school too, are fundamentally different from those in the US. As such, there are practical reasons why interdisciplinarity is difficult to achieve in the English context, far beyond questions of educational will. To ask why English degrees can't be more like US degrees, as some liberal arts advocates do, is a bit like asking why custard creams can't be more like peanut brittle. It's because the ingredients are different.

The chapter finally turns to one of the main ways in which those designing liberal arts degrees seek to achieve interdisciplinarity when students take such disparate disciplinary combinations: the core module. Such modules seek to bring together otherwise potentially fragmentary degrees, and they often try to do so through a highly applied approach, charging students with solving, as in the epigraph, some so-far-intractable social problems. This applied approach can be connected to a much broader move towards context-dependent (or even 'real-world') learning, where education is thought to happen best through concrete examples.

Importantly, this context-dependent or applied approach can be conceptualised as a pedagogical *tool*, providing an accessible route to later context-independent knowledge that can be moved *between* contexts (Rata, 2016), or, conversely, valued as an end in itself and as an implied critique of 'pure' or abstract knowledge more commonly associated with disciplines. I argue that while concrete application may be a route to student understanding in lots of educational contexts, if such application does not present a clear explanation of how to apply that knowledge to *new* problems, independently identified, it may in fact lead to a narrowing, rather than a broadening, of intellectual horizons (Wheelahan, 2007). While the hyper-interdisciplinary impulse tries to smooth over tensions like this, I interpret students' critical comments as attempts to disentangle hyper-interdisciplinary claims from a more measured belief in what Moore (2011) calls *routine* interdisciplinarity.

The problem with disciplines: contingency and falsehood

Before beginning to discuss in more detail how liberal arts degrees are posited as *solutions* to the problem of disciplines later in the chapter, this first section briefly describes how promotional websites, academics and students conceptualise disciplines as problematic. Crucially, for a large number of participants (though by no means all), disciplines could be understood as inherently narrow and therefore as leading to the narrow*ing* of horizons. Third-year student Jen, who was completing her degree at a modern institution where the liberal arts degree was highly interdisciplinary, rather than merely multidisciplinary, contrasted this approach with the narrowness of a single disciplinary mode:

> 'We'd look at [a topic] through different philosophical lenses, where it's sort of medicine, or engineering, or poetry, or whatever, and it would give us a real sort of holistic education of something that would otherwise have been a very narrow perspective of a single narrative. We're able to take the breadth of that and make it what we will.' (Jen, third-year student, modern)

As we will see in a subsequent section, in England in particular, there is a clear link between the discipline and the department, and some students tied in their criticism of disciplines to the regressive nature of departments, which liberal arts degrees were battling. Third-year student Asif explained the difficulties faced by those at his old institution who were trying to break down such barriers: "The departments just stay – they just try to keep to their own a bit. So, I think [liberal arts] do as good a job as they can, trying to sort that out. But I think some departments are just quite closed off."

The specific ways that holism and integration are framed by students here give a slightly moral character to the oft-heard critique of disciplines. The text on promotional websites, as well as the words of senior academics, on the other hand, sometimes made a much stronger claim: that the diverse nature of disciplines and, crucially, their changeability over time mean that they are not reliable institutional structures for us to put store in at all. Here, disciplines' historical contingency is stressed in order to foreground their constructed and transitory nature, suggesting a future that will have moved beyond them: 'It is important to bear in mind that the disciplines are not set in stone. Indeed, over history they change frequently; some come and go and some are unrecognisable from 100 or even 30 years ago' (website, old). Post-war dean of faculty Tim, who distinguished between 'mono-disciplines' and more interdisciplinary areas of study, connected his lack of attachment to the former with their historical impermanence:

Tim: Would I shed a tear for the mono-disciplines? No.
Kathryn: No?
Tim: Mono-disciplines have been around in most cases for less than a hundred years? Sociology only for fifty years?[1]

In examples like this, there is a suggestion that if something is historically specific, it is therefore arbitrary, useless or even suspect, or 'that for knowledge to be knowledge it must be outside history' (Young, 2008: 3). Indeed, interdisciplinary impulses often arise via a distrust of disciplines (though they need not do so), which goes well beyond acknowledgement of contingency to stress, as in early 1970s' 'transdisciplinary' optimism, that it is only by moving beyond the shackles of the disciplinary past that we can get to a better future (Bernstein, 2015).

This high-positivist belief that contingency itself is suspect leads to an idea that *any* attempt to divide up the world into meaningful units is inherently regressive, as it moves us away from 'true' knowledge, which is ahistorical and even indistinguishable from the 'real world', as in this example from a liberal arts promotional website: 'knowledge is often split into separate "disciplines" such as those in the sciences, maths, history, geography, literature and art. However, true knowledge does not recognise these boundaries; the world is complex, interconnected and networked' (website, post-war).

While we will go on to discuss those that offered interesting critiques of extreme interdisciplinary ideas like these, some students did echo this belief more commonly seen on promotional websites and heard from senior academics. Here too, disciplinary divisions were felt to be arbitrary, especially given the ways that each discipline broke off into separate subdisciplines, looking suspiciously like each other. For Konstantina, a second-year student with a voracious appetite for modules across the sciences, social sciences, humanities and arts at her old university:

---

[1] Tim tended to use sociology specifically as an example when discussing the 'mono-disciplines'. For further reflections on this, see note 1 to Chapter 5.

'Some of the modules in anthropology are political anthropology, economic anthropology, biological anthropology. Then, if you go to geography, it's cultural geography, political geography, economic geography. And then, if you go to politics, we have history of politics, political philosophy. So, you kind of realise it's a mess, you know? They are all kind of the same. ... What I'm trying to say is if an anthropology student did some politics and economics and philosophy and psychology and geography modules, as I have done, they would realise that it's all the same really. ... And at the end, you're like, "Why do we have disciplines anyway?"'

Clearly, liberal arts degrees are partially being imagined as ways precisely to break down such divisions. As Konstantina notes, studying an interdisciplinary degree has led her to question the value of disciplinary groupings that she has come to view as arbitrary if not downright obfuscatory. Indeed, liberal arts degrees seem ideally placed to break down such divisions. In the next section, we will turn to the question of how successful those involved in the liberal arts consider them to be at doing so.

The Build-a-Bear degree? Tensions of choice and progression

One important question to ask about any interdisciplinary initiative is whether it is interdisciplinary or, in fact, *multi*disciplinary. That is to say, does study on a particular liberal arts degree integrate disciplinary study so that different disciplines speak to one another, or rather does it facilitate the study of multiple subjects without much integration, being more akin to a joint-honours course?

As we might expect, there is a significant amount of variety between degrees on this score. Some degrees are promoted largely according to the market value of individual choice, which tends to stress disciplines as discrete units to be picked and mixed through the conduit of individually selected modules. Here, what matters is the scale of optionality, rather than ideas about integration. Since I began researching English liberal arts degrees in 2016, this pick-and-mix narrative, at least in its most straightforward guise, seems to have abated on promotional websites, with greater emphasis now placed on the importance of coherence and integration, especially through core modules.

Some students in interviews did indeed have a strong sense of interdisciplinarity as distinct from multidisciplinarity, and wished to integrate their studies into a coherent whole. Second-year student Victoria, for instance, had chosen her liberal arts degree at an old university in order to bring insights from chemistry and maths together in a coherent way:

'But it wasn't like I wanted to study more than one thing because I couldn't make up my mind, which is definitely what a lot of people think when you say "liberal arts". It was just that I liked all these subjects and the idea of bringing them all together into, like, saying, "I'm going to take all of these things and bring them all together to something new", is much more interesting to me to studying them as isolated things.'

While institutional websites increasingly stress a holistic education of the type Victoria values, however, many students remain at least partially motivated by individual choice and the pick-and-mix approach. For Logan, a US student just completing his degree at a private institution, one difference between his own course and the liberal arts degrees with which he was familiar back home was the lack of distribution requirements, meaning that he was able to focus on the specific modules that interested him: "I didn't really run out of the country just to avoid the math teacher; it wasn't that bad. But it would've been on the list." An important corollary to market values of choice was the notion of a multidisciplinary degree as a way of delaying a decision considered too difficult at the end of school, as Logan went on to explain: "The reason why I chose a liberal arts degree was 'cause I wasn't sure what I was going to want to do career-wise in high school, so I chose instead to do something that was very wide in focus, and I'd be able to narrow it down later."

For a number of students who *themselves* sought an integrated and interdisciplinary education, individualist choice motivations remained valid for their fellow students. Phoebe was just finishing their degree at a post-war institution and had followed a thread of cognate humanities disciplines throughout. Yet, it was completely reasonable to them that a friend described it as a Build-a-Bear degree: "You can choose where you want the heart from; you can choose where you want the skin; you can choose, you know – you can construct it yourself." For others still, interdisciplinarity was about "applying techniques from one discipline to problems in another", as third-year student Jessica explained. This is a specific notion of interdisciplinarity that actually preserves the distinction between the disciplines. Studying at an old institution, Jessica was focusing on English and maths, apparently very different disciplines that she thought were actually "more similar than people realise".

Some of those students who believed in the tenets of interdisciplinarity, however, expressed their reservations about how interdisciplinary their degree was in practice. Devendra, a fourth-year student at an old institution, had held high hopes for the chance to integrate the subjects that interested him though a liberal arts degree. Coming to the end of his studies, he reflected that "it feels like more of a multidisciplinary degree; so, I feel like more of a dual-honours student than I do an interdisciplinary student. So, I see very little crossover between chemistry and philosophy, and virtually no opportunity to explore the interface between the two" (Devendra, fourth-year student, old). Academic Alan, a dean at a modern institution, explained at a structural level what the problem was:

Alan: It's just that you've got, you know, a sociology Lego brick and a biology Lego brick. The student ends up multicoloured, but the modules aren't.
Kathryn: But the units are completely discrete.
Alan: The units are still yellow and green or whatever. [Pause.] No. I was gonna pursue the analogy but it's too boring.

Alan's Lego analogy helps us to see very clearly a much broader issue at stake in English higher education today: modularisation. In a highly modularised system, individual course units are understood as discrete from one another. Each individual student may pick and choose between such modules, without the particular edifice the student is building as a whole making any difference to the units themselves, or to how they are taught.

However, while English higher education has clearly become *more* modularised over the last 30 years (Ainley, 2016b), this move towards choice or market values remains entangled with a strong sense of progression from one stage to the next. This concern might be understood as an industrial value, associated with rigour and maintaining standards. It means that, in practice, many modules retain prerequisites, or requirements that students must have passed a preceding module before they can enrol onto the next. This tension between choice and progression begins not when students start their undergraduate degrees, but long before, as we will see in the next section.

For some senior academics, old-fashioned notions of progression like this were hindering English institutions from really being able to take on what is valuable about the US system. Alan, now a dean at a modern institution but with experience teaching on US-style degrees at private institutions, went on to criticise the English system in this regard: "But the American notion that basically you have an open entry to the freshman stage and the ability, right through, to mix levels of module is really alien to the UK mentality I think" (Alan, dean, modern). However, for other, more junior staff, there was a real *academic* logic to concerns about progression. Programme director Adrian was alive to the market logic of choice, but also sympathetic to the concerns of academics at his post-war university about progression. Rather than criticising the latter as mere disciplinary fustiness, he observed that there was a real tension here:

'And again, sort of a tension between wanting to give students complete freedom (you know, just, "Here's the module catalogue and anything you want to do you can go and do") against a lot of concerns from departments about having students who don't know anything about anything suddenly deciding they want to do nuclear physics in the final year.'[2]

The tension between the individualist free-choice narrative and concerns with progression was also felt keenly by a lot of students. Academic advisers had a particular role in helping students to navigate this complex terrain, especially when it came to keeping future disciplinary options open. Some advisers, seemingly encouraged to think of liberal arts degrees as governed by principles of choice, were reportedly reluctant to advise on progression routes, instead preferring to sign off module choices if it was what the student had chosen. Second-year student Mathilde, studying at an old university, had felt that her academic adviser had taken this approach, prioritising choice over progression and coherence. This felt good in the moment, but she sometimes felt that "They should be more direct rather than just signing the list and telling us it's fine. I think it would be a very good thing." Caught between modularisation, with its conceptualisation of education as market commodity, and progression as the mainstay of the English single-subject degree tradition, academic advisers find themselves in the crossfire of a very specific tension at the heart of English liberal arts degrees, to which we will now turn.

How England is not like the US: a partial list

'I mean, I've not had anybody sort of, you know, say – as far as I know – in a board of studies or anything, "Well it's completely ridiculous to do liberal arts and sciences; we should stick with the disciplines." Never. Never. On the contrary, everyone's been very happy to allow us to do it, but then when the practicalities start getting in the way, they don't start saying, "Well, it's wrong to do the liberal arts"; they say, "It's just too complicated."' (Tim, dean, post-war)

In the preceding quotation, Tim is relating some of the problems that he faced in making a liberal arts degree work in practice. He suggests that rather than pedagogical reasons or mere disciplinary old-fashionedness, it is practical constraints that constitute a major impediment to making liberal arts degrees work. Indeed, in the context of the degree he helped to institute as dean at his post-war university, they were a factor in its demise.

---

[2] Adrian's reference to nuclear physics points towards an important difference: that even very advanced humanities and social science courses are perceived as appropriate for generalists in ways that the natural and physical sciences are not.

While I would suggest that the reason we have ended up with the particular institutional configurations we have is not completely divorced from our *ideas* about education (Hogan, 2012), it can often be practical constraints that bog us down in the here and now. Recent liberal arts initiatives are hardly the first to try to broaden out from the traditional, single-discipline undergraduate degree, and earlier attempts (for instance, at innovative post-war universities like Keele and Kent) also struggled to bed in for infrastructural reasons. Of course, US institutions have concerns about final-year students wanting to study nuclear physics too, as well as systems to deal with this, including prerequisites. However, our ability to deal with these tensions well has to do with the whole educational infrastructure in the national context, not just in higher education, but at school too.

In this section, we will address ourselves to two key ways in which the English higher education system makes the instigation and management of liberal arts degrees extremely difficult: first, the very strong connection between single-subject degrees and departments; and, second, specific ideas about progression and specialisation. Both ideas have already been touched on in this chapter but will be spelled out further here, with a particular view to understanding infrastructural constraints.

First, English higher education is premised on a close correlation between the *degree* and the *department*. That is to say, while joint-honours degrees and elective modules certainly exist, universities are premised upon the notion that students have a departmental home and that at least half of their degree will be comprised of modules from that department. Departments, then, tend to proceed as if students are fundamentally 'theirs' (an English student; a maths student) and do not always communicate about how to teach joint-honours students, much less those taking the liberal arts. The departments proceed as if any difficulties thrown up by the decision to take a wacky degree were the students' own to sort out – or that's how it felt to students. As we saw in the previous section, for instance, third-year student Jessica was specialising in English and maths at her old institution. Yet, the fundamental differences of time management between the disciplines were not appreciated by the departments. While maths provides a large number of contact hours with less individual study, English is the reverse, so that she found herself with novels to read and essays to write every week, on top of a large number of maths lectures. Matters as prosaic as timetabling, especially of ad hoc events, could be an especial challenge.[3]

---

[3] If module convenors are looking, as we will see later, for large-scale wicked problems to try to solve through the liberal arts approach, university timetabling is surely one of the wickedest.

The link between the discipline and the department is only further exacerbated by procedures like the Research Excellence Framework (the national research audit), into which all members of a department are often submitted under one disciplinary category. This is despite the fact that, on the ground, many departments with a clear disciplinary name are in fact multidisciplinary in practice, and academics don't always identify clearly with their departmental name either (Chandler and Davidson, 2009). Programme director Hélène now worked in a language department at a post-war university but had experience studying and teaching at a range of institutions. Like other academics I talked to in area studies, in particular, she noted a mismatch between her institutional home and her disciplinary identity:

Kathryn: Do you say you're a language scholar, or … ?
Hélène: No. I say more really research-wise, I'm a historian.
Kathryn: Okay. You would situate yourself as a historian.
Hélène: Yep.
Kathryn: Have you ever worked in a history department?
Hélène: Never! [Both laugh.]

While there are clearly strong links between disciplines, departments and degrees in the US system, they are not conflated in quite the same way. In particular, the strongly modularised and elective system in many US institutions means that it has been possible, at least historically, for a large number of small programmes to emerge. These don't necessarily supply full majors, but can provide electives; in particular, 101 modules for entry-level students (Messer-Davidow, 2002). While some small programmes are increasingly at risk of closure in the US, this historical difference (the existence of departments that do not run full degrees) is important. In the English case, the link between the department and the degree has a long precedent, and it persists. For example, *departments* are often scrutinised by management according to how many students study their disciplinary *degrees*. Liberal arts courses can even be pursued partially as a way to disrupt this department–degree link in the context of departmental closures, as post-war programme director Adrian explained:

'And it was also a way of entangling different disciplines together that are sort of seen, in institutional terms – this was a way maybe to get some more bodies on the ground and also to make it harder to separate out particular disciplines that might be at risk. 'Cause at the point that this was happening, the university was, it turned out, starting to think about its size and shape.'[4]

---

[4] 'Size and shape' is a well-known and much-derided management term for compulsory redundancies via institutional restructuring. At one institution I worked at,

'Entangling' disciplines together is, then, a way of *disentangling* them from their disciplinary degrees and arguing for a more careful way of accounting for student numbers than simplistic market formulas.

The second key way in which the English higher education infrastructure differs from that of the US is the approach to specialisation and progression. While specialisation over time is a key feature of both systems, the how and, crucially, *when* are quite different. In the US, specialisation generally happens *over the course* of a four-year undergraduate degree, often with a clear difference between the first two and the second two years. (The first two characterised by more general education, which may be taught at an altogether different institution, such as a community college). Historically, there has also been a greater emphasis on postgraduate work as the site for specialist, especially vocational, training. Jen, coming to the end of her studies at a modern institution, alluded to something closer to the US system when she recounted: "One of my friends on the degree was like, 'Everyone should do a liberal arts degree and then decide what they want to do at university.'"

This is markedly different from the usual English trajectory, where the curriculum is reduced to around ten subjects at the age of 14, to around three subjects at 16 for those who stay in academic education and, finally, to one (or two) subjects for those who pursue undergraduate study. We can't understand the highly specialised nature of English degrees, then, without going back to school and, especially, looking at what happens at A level, when many 16-year-olds choose around three subjects to study in depth (though there are a range of alternatives, including more vocational qualifications and, as we will see later, the broader international baccalaureate).

Many students I talked to, as we might expect from people who had chosen an interdisciplinary degree, had found choosing three subjects at A level extremely hard. Fourth-year student Phoebe, studying at a post-war university, was fairly typical in this regard: "When I had to choose my A levels, I found it really difficult 'cause I wanted to do about nine different things." In particular, some students felt pressed to make choices that were deemed cogent by teachers, such teachers holding what students now perceived to be old-fashioned ideas about those subjects that could be combined fruitfully or that would appeal to university selectors. Like Phoebe, Victoria (in the second year of her degree at an old institution) had struggled to select from the many subjects she enjoyed and was good at, eventually deferring to her teachers: "I was basically strongly advised to take geography because it linked more with the other subjects I was doing. So, that was definitely the point at which they were like, 'You're doing sciences

---

management had taken to calling it 'shape and size' instead, which was, thankfully, completely different.

now, not art.'" Indeed, the various challenges associated with taking A levels across the arts and sciences has led some higher education institutions, which had previously asked for this breadth as an entry requirement, to drop it from their selection criteria.

In a sense, to focus on breadth at degree level is, in clear contrast to the US system, to go *backward* from school, which has encouraged students to specialise quite far by the age of 18. Some academics talked about the liberal arts as a kind of *unlearning* from school, rather than a progression. Meanwhile, those with personal experience of broader school and university curricula did not think that some features of certain liberal arts approaches in the US, like a common core of general education for all students, would ever be possible within the English system. Indeed, those who had received their own educations in systems that maintained breadth for much longer were generally more realistic about what could be achieved, and sustained, within an English university. They were particularly clear about the difficulties of incorporating the natural and physical sciences given the specific ideas of specialisation and progression built into the system. Larry, a dean involved in initiating the liberal arts degree at his old university, and who had himself studied a liberal arts degree in North America, had never seriously entertained the idea that students would be able to take science: "The challenge of just getting it off the ground in the arts context was challenging enough. To add a science element, I couldn't even see where to start really because we don't really have general science here." By contrast, staff at another university had been highly ambitious, and the difficulties of sustaining such a model across faculties had been one reason for the degree's demise. As Ellie, a second-year student at a different old institution, told me, while the degree was in arts *and sciences*, most students did very little science indeed, and when talking casually about the degree, "'sciences' kind of often falls off".

What Larry refers to as general science is that idea of the entry-level module or 101 touched on earlier. Since *all* students in the US are significantly more interdisciplinary than most students in England, and because of distribution requirements demanding that a broad range of subjects is taken before specialisation occurs, entry-level modules are a necessity for the functioning of that system. This is very different from having to create such modules from scratch for a small group of interdisciplinarily minded students.

The assumption from departments, as we have seen, is often that students will be disciplinary specialists, and this creates particular problems for liberal arts students. We note this especially in expectations about high-level discipline-specific skills that single-honours students receive training in and liberal arts students do not. As we also saw earlier, Devendra, coming to the end of his degree at an old institution, felt that the different disciplines he was interested in had not been brought into dialogue on his course. As well as noting this limitation on the intellectual level, he also recounted difficulties at the level of departmental expectations and skills:

'So, they had a module called X, which covered a lot of the calculations and sort of methods that they would have to do for lab reports, something that wasn't available to me. I was quite confused when I started getting really low marks only to find out that it was something that everybody else had been taught.'

As we will see in Chapter 3, many students work hard to cover this ground for themselves and see the difficulty of this process as one of the things that makes the degree valuable. On the other hand, the creation of 101s could lead to a *lack* of challenge: Jessica, the advanced maths student we met earlier, for instance, was expected to take an entry-level quantitative methods course as part of her core curriculum. The combination of these various infrastructural issues could lead to student dissatisfaction, and academics often felt like, as post-war programme director Hélène put it, "the bad cop".

Given the apparent mismatch between the specialisation of A levels and the breadth of the liberal arts, many academics and students noted that a far better preparation for an interdisciplinary degree was in fact the international baccalaureate diploma programme. Offering a common educational core stressing critical thinking and a wider breadth of subjects, including compulsory maths and a foreign language, the international baccalaureate more closely resembles both the US high-school diploma and the English liberal arts degree. This qualification's pertinence to the liberal arts degree was mentioned on websites, by academics and by students alike. Ben, in his second year of a liberal arts degree at a post-war university, felt that the students who had taken the international baccalaureate on his course were better prepared and generally seemed more *educated* than himself, having taken A levels: "And, you know, if you look at the IB [international baccalaureate] it's – it looks almost like the perfect precursor to a liberal arts degree." Dean Tim likewise noted that many of the liberal arts students at his post-war institution were well prepared for their degree because "a lot of them IB'd, so they would have studied a little bit of these things at a relatively high level at school or something. But, obviously, if you're focusing on three A levels, you know, three disciplines, you're obviously going to be highly specialising." Institutions' promotional websites also sometimes flagged the link: 'At [this institution,] we recognise the high level of academic achievement required to succeed in the broad IB curriculum. We are impressed by current students who studied the IB and are delighted to receive applications from IB students' (website, private).

Importantly, many students who had studied the international baccalaureate connected its similarity to the liberal arts to the difficulty of both educational modes, in comparison to A levels. In the case of the international baccalaureate, this was often related to the relatively high number of contact hours, in comparison to the in-class workload of A-levelling peers. Marta, now in her second year at an old university, had had the choice to study either A levels or the international baccalaureate at her private school, and although it had been a relatively easy choice for her to take the latter because she was interested in so many subjects, she noted this difference in difficulty: "In the IB, you get a really, really big workload in comparison to A level students, just because you're studying double the amount of subjects and you have a lot more contact hours and less time to spend on your work."

The international baccalaureate is, as in Marta's case, more likely to be available to students at private schools (Resnik, 2012). Indeed, many of the state-educated students I met had not heard of the qualification until coming to university. High contact hours and highly directional teaching are often a feature of private schooling, and while the students who have received these often equate them with educational quality, this experience can contribute to some private school pupils' difficulties when they encounter the more autonomous learning style favoured by universities – a learning style to which state school pupils are generally already accustomed (Bathmaker et al, 2016). In Chapter 6, we will probe in significantly more detail this relationship between educational breadth, educational *intimacy* and social class.

This discussion of some of the infrastructural constraints around implementing liberal arts degrees has demonstrated that we need not only to consider what happens at the university level, but also connect this to what happens in schools. As we have seen, implementing a liberal arts degree is not merely about educational beliefs, but must be made to work in settings where the approach often goes against the infrastructural grain. In the following section, we turn to one of the means liberal arts advocates use to create an educational setting that is more suited to the liberal arts approach: the core module.

The application of what? Problems with problem-based learning

> At [this university], we've reimagined what Liberal Arts education means for the twenty-first century by focusing on problems, not disciplines. (Website, post-war)

This chapter has so far examined both the problems with disciplines as conceptualised by liberal arts advocates and the difficulties of achieving interdisciplinarity in a degree within the English system given the general approach to specialisation and progression in higher education, as well as at school. This section examines one of the key ways that liberal arts degrees seek to achieve interdisciplinarity (as opposed to multidisciplinarity) in this context: core modules – in particular, those that take an applied approach to specific, concrete problems. Here, I will argue that there is an important difference between interdisciplinarity and *trans*-disciplinarity, or, perhaps, following Rob Moore (2011), between routine interdisciplinarity and hyper-interdisciplinarity. While the former is a fairly everyday experience of university life (for instance, when academics from different disciplines work together on a research project), trans-disciplinarity, or hyper-interdisciplinarity, entails a more normative belief about disciplines as problematic (Bernstein, 2015). I will argue that core, applied modules, as described on websites, tend to entangle routine and hyper-interdisciplinarity together; for instance, by conflating the interdisciplinary research team with the lone, interdisciplinary undergraduate. This takes the highly individualist value of pursuing your interest wherever it leads and knots it in with the collectivist nature of professional research as it is actually practised. Through their often gentle critiques of these modules and the hyper-interdisciplinarity they promote, students seek to disentangle it from a routine interdisciplinarity that they find truly valuable.

As we have already seen in this chapter, various restrictions make it difficult to facilitate interdisciplinarity, as opposed to the multidisciplinarity that characterises joint-honours degrees, in English higher education. One difference between most joint-honours courses and liberal arts degrees, however, is that the latter almost always contain bespoke core modules taken only by liberal arts students, which are taken irrespective of the constituent disciplines of each student's degree. Precisely because each liberal arts student is studying a diverse range of subjects, though, creating cogent and relevant core modules can prove a challenge. The result can be highly abstract modules about critical thinking, epistemology or interdisciplinarity itself, and while students can sometimes see the benefit of such courses after the fact, their value is not always immediately obvious. At the end of her first year, Veronika summed up what she thought was the feeling of many of her peers at an old university: "We couldn't quite pinpoint what the purpose of that [core] module was because it felt very abstract."

One way of designing core modules that are relevant to students taking a wide range of subjects without remaining at a highly abstract level is to go precisely the other way and focus on application. Here, the idea is that students can bring their varied expertise to examine concrete, 'real-world' issues or problems, often in groups. Some degrees specifically follow the model of problem-based learning here: a pedagogical approach first developed in the 1960s at McMaster medical school in Canada as a way to get students to practise actively what they would have to do as doctors (that is, diagnose patients' problems). Presented with a complex range of symptoms, students would have to first identify the gaps in their own knowledge and then fill those gaps in order to come to a diagnosis (Savery, 2015). While core courses at many institutions do not follow the specific approach developed at McMaster, they often do take this general pedagogical style of presenting students with a specific, 'real-world' scenario and asking them to solve it.

Such a post-disciplinary approach has been promoted by, for instance, the Organisation for Economic Co-operation and Development as 'true' knowledge finally freed from the false logic of the disciplines (Hughson and Wood, 2022). Often, the way that such applied and 'real-world' learning is presented on institutions' websites has a moral character, moving us away from the abstract irrelevance of the disciplines and towards 'the questions that matter' (website, post-war). Even where problems with a less material basis (such as ones about emotions or indeed about learning itself) are discussed, these remain separate from questions about the 'real world' ('real' here seemingly a synonym for physical):

> Many of the world's great problems require an interdisciplinary approach to solve them. This is true of problems in the 'real world' – e.g. problems to do with health, politics, engineering or cities – but also important intellectual problems – e.g. the relation between reasoning and emotion, the study of culture and identity, the link between music and learning. (Website, old)

Why questions about emotions, identity and music should be considered unreal is not made clear; Stefan Collini (2012: 145) has remarked that such a sparse conception of the real world is 'obviously the brainchild of cloistered businessmen, living in their ivory factories and out of touch with the kinds of things that matter to ordinary people like you and me. They should get out more.'

As in the preceding quotation from an institutional website, the type of questions to be solved by the interdisciplinary, applied approach tend to be massive, global and complete (often captured by a short phrase as one coherent problem), rather than local, specific or partial: 'you will investigate complex challenges such as childhood obesity, plastic pollution, genome editing, and knife crime' (website, private). Such topics are sometimes framed as 'wicked problems'; that is, issues so complex and, well, if not exactly intractable, then extremely difficult to tract that they require a very complete, interdisciplinary approach, capable of looking at the problem from every conceivable side.

Perhaps unsurprisingly, it is difficult to do such expansive problems justice within the confines of a core undergraduate module:

> Through your research, you will consider what kind of change you seek (e.g. individual attitudes or access to resources), what precedents there are, who the stakeholders are and what kind of power is involved, what strategies could bring about change and how to measure the effectiveness of the change you seek. The class meets for two hours every week. (Website, old)

Equally unsurprisingly, students sometimes found such pedagogical approaches a challenge. There is a lot being asked of (often first-year) students in modules like this, and the learning outcomes and assessment criteria could be simultaneously expansive and unclear. While Alina, just finishing her first year at an old institution, for example, ultimately found her problem-based module rewarding, she also found the range of requirements difficult to meet:

> 'It was definitely difficult to do, especially in so few words, to really – because you had to – obviously there was no requirement as to what kind of reading you had to include, so it was kind of difficult to sort of get it together into something that answered the question and that also related appropriately to all the different requirements.'

The application of problem-based learning techniques to these very large problems may present challenges for students partially because of a lack of clarity about what it means for something to actually *be* a problem. Problem-based learning in its strict McMaster form was designed as a means to diagnose cancer; yet, in some core liberal arts modules, it is seemingly being used more like a means of *eradicating* cancer. While we might refer to both the diagnosis and the eradication of cancer as 'problems' in everyday life, they are in fact very different sorts of problem. Diagnosis is a small-scale, applied, local problem, and it generally has a single, correct answer. (Of course, this doesn't make diagnosing cancer a simple matter.) Eradicating cancer, on the other hand, is a very big sort of problem requiring both basic and applied research, and is better seen as an incremental build-up of answers to many smaller questions tackled by many different specialists over many years.

Perhaps some of the difficulties students experience with problem-based learning relate to the fact that they are being asked to answer the latter type of problem as if it were like the former. This also relates to a general lack of clarity at times about whether problem-based learning is precisely that – that is, a pedagogical tool that uses simulations to help students *learn* something beyond the specific case – or, conversely, whether it is in fact the correct way to proceed in professional research. The latter, hyper-interdisciplinary approach appears to imagine that the very different types of expertise held by a medical doctor and a research scientist are the same (Collins and Evans, 2007), and to forget the importance of basic research in the progression of knowledge (Flexner, 2017).

The instrumentalist treatment of large and complex problems as if they require only technical solutions can be seen in the following example explaining why an interdisciplinary approach is crucial for society's progress:

> How do we end world poverty by 2030? To begin to answer this question from within the university, we have to bring biologists

together with sociologists, political scientists with climatologists, and historians with economists. We have to train researchers to think in new ways, and put them together with activists and politicians able to connect theory and practice. (Website, post-war)

At first blush, this appears a suitably complex solution to a complex problem. Yet, by treating politicians as just another group with some particular technical competence (the practical application of theory), it in fact sidesteps what makes the problem intractable in the first place. World poverty is a consequence of inequity and injustice; in short, it has to do with power. And while the social scientists around this (massive) imaginary table will no doubt mention that interpretation as part of their technical expertise, if it were simply a matter of getting politicians to understand and then connect this theory to practice, wouldn't we have solved world poverty some time ago? To extend the preceding metaphor, we may be able to diagnose the problem using technical expertise in this way, but there is no reason for politicians to act against their own interests in order to eradicate it. We will need to go well beyond a technical understanding in order to get to grips with the complexity of this particular problem.

This example throws up a second logical point: the assumption that sociologists, climatologists and the rest actually exist. But where have such disciplinary specialists come from? Examples like this are given on liberal arts websites in order to make the case for interdisciplinarity at the undergraduate level. Yet, the participants in the interdisciplinary conversations invoked are already disciplinary experts. This is a blurring of the distinction between the interdisciplinary team of disciplinary specialists and the individual interdisciplinarian, which Roger Shattuck (1973) observed as a problem for interdisciplinary degrees 50 years ago. Entangling these together allows very big claims to be made for what can be achieved through undergraduate study alone.

On some core, problem-based modules, students are treated as individual experts who can bring their disciplinary knowledge to bear on a concrete case. Here, students learn from one another's disciplinary expertise, rather than being positioned as interdisciplinary (or trans-disciplinary) experts themselves: 'Each member of the group will provide disciplinary expertise and will teach a seminar to the rest of the research group' (website, old). There are, however, lots of converse arguments that make the case for the interdisciplinary *individual*. The following example is arguing for interdisciplinary professional research to be carried out by one person, though in the context of explaining the value of interdisciplinarity at the undergraduate level:

> Let's say we want to find out why a particular disease is spreading among a community. You need to know about the disease, so you need

some aspects of biomedicine. If the disease reoccurs at different times and in different places, you may need to use statistics and computer modelling to understand better how it is spreading. You may notice that the disease spreads more where people live in close communities or have a particular diet. So you may need to investigate the economics or politics of the situation that obliges people to live in a certain way. Finally, if the disease is concentrated in a non-English-speaking country, you may need a non-English language to understand properly what is going on. Thus, for a full understanding, you may need to combine the subjects of Biomedicine, Computer Modelling, Economics, Politics, and a foreign language. (Website, old)

We may wonder quite how efficient this highly individualist formulation of interdisciplinarity is likely to be. Wouldn't I be better off getting a computer modeller or language specialist on to my team, rather than trying to learn these skills from scratch? And how much time do I have to acquire these complex proficiencies, when developing biomedical expertise is itself nothing to be sniffed at? We might also wonder whether this talented individual can now only do biomedical research in countries that speak the language in which they are now proficient – or should they perhaps learn a new language for each project? Crucially, should this person have known that this was the specific research project they wanted to conduct when they began their undergraduate studies? These are facetious questions, but the broader point is that this highly individualist way of imagining interdisciplinarity denies the collective nature of much research. It also sidesteps the question of *how* expertise is developed (generally very slowly and in painstaking and labour-intensive ways) before we can get to the point of considering 'inter-ing' anything (Barrett, 2012). While acknowledgement of this problem is present on some institutional websites ('Moving unthinkingly to a problem-based approach risks losing the focus that allows expertise to develop' [website, private]), most entangle these values in a much more celebratory way.

This is part of a perennial tension between depth and breadth that plagues the liberal arts. Promotional websites sometimes present the liberal arts as in fact the solution to this problem, as they offer both breadth (of disciplines) and depth (through application). Students too recounted being told this. With some scepticism, second-year student Victoria described a visit to her old university's open day, where "they were speaking about, 'Yes, there's – you gain greater breadth', but they try and have it that you have depth in, like, your specific area."

Some students more explicitly doubted the extent to which this depth was really possible, especially in the context of core modules. Asif, now going into his final year, discussed a compulsory 101 course that all liberal arts students at his old university had had to take, irrespective of their pre-existing expertise (likely to be significant in the case of A level graduates at an elite university):

> 'They were like, "We want this to be accessible to generalists", even though there are a lot of really good mathematicians on our course. So, they don't teach enough maths that you can go out and research something, or look into the papers that well. You just have to look into papers about papers, or examples about papers.'

As in this instance, the tendency to focus on concrete application, rather than skills, was particularly criticised by students in relation to first-year core modules. Bianca, a third-year student at an old institution, on the other hand, related the issue to the liberal arts and preparation for work more broadly. She had a keen interest in astrophysics and had considered an academic career in the field. While applied learning is often presented as about accessing the real world, however, for Bianca, one layer of reality at least was absent from such a picture:

> 'I think it's a very different thing to want to study it because you think it's interesting, or you like the idea of how you could possibly time travel, or black holes or something like that. It's a different story to sitting in the lab and doing maths the whole day!'

Bianca alludes to the fact that any application is an application *of something*, and this more fundamental (disciplinary, specialist) work, while sometimes presented as stuffy, or even technicist and trivial, cannot really be avoided if we wish to come to a realistic picture of what academic work entails.

There appears to be something contradictory about relating the highly specialised and applied form of expertise extolled as individual interdisciplinarity here to the liberal arts given that, in the US, one of the only broadly agreed-upon definitions of liberal education is that it is not applied (Brewer, 2018). However, there are multiple understandings one can take from the 'general' in general education, and while the highly specialised and applied approach that problem-based learning takes clearly does not tie in with the idea of non-applied study, it comes much closer to what Bruce Kimball (1986) refers to as 'individualist' general education; that is, where every individual is free to select the education that suits their interests and aims. This is a market-based conception and, on one level, was deeply attractive to students I talked to. However, as Bianca and others suggest, one aspect of the real world (and quite a significant one) is deferred gratification: often, we can only get to what we want via things we do not. In order to be able to speak Italian on my holiday (something I want), I have to do Italian exercises every day before I go (something I really, really can't be bothered to do). Paradoxically, the freedom to choose whatever we want cannot get us many of the things we desire.

Thus, while the hyper-interdisciplinary narrative often, as at the beginning of this chapter, stresses the narrowness of disciplinary structures as against the breadth of interdisciplinarity, the particular model of interdisciplinary education that many liberal arts students in England receive in their core modules (the application of different types of expertise to one specific, concrete problem) can be said to actually *narrow* one's horizons. For instance, while a degree in physics presents opportunities to, later, apply that knowledge to a wide range of interesting problems (in a dissertation, postgraduate study or at work), an undergraduate career spent trying to 'solve climate change' may actually narrow one's conversations and the scope to address different sorts of problems.

If application (for instance, investigating black holes) is conceived of as actually *doing* research and seeking to solve a problem (as it is often presented on websites), why would first-year undergraduates be the ones to do it? As Larry, a liberal arts instigator at an old university, pointed out: "The real depth, if you're going to be a real specialist, is probably going to come at postgraduate level anyway." If, on the other hand, applied learning is a pedagogical device designed to get students *somewhere else*, rather than being an end in itself (for example, using black holes as a hook to hang the teaching of general relativity upon), disentangling this second meaning from its more hyperbolic cousin seems important for students (Rata, 2016).

Students often maintained a distinction between hyper-interdisciplinarity and routine interdisciplinarity in their discussions, and this was especially clear for those nearing the end of their degrees. The interview was a chance to cast a sceptical (and frequently humorous) eye over parts of the endeavour, while remaining absolutely committed to other aspects. For these students, the questions of when interdisciplinarity should begin and what should precede it were central.

Jessica, now at the end of her degree at one old institution and about to embark on interdisciplinary postgraduate work at another, was convinced of the importance of interdisciplinary work *after* disciplinary knowledge had been meaningfully acquired: "I do think that the ability to think like that is necessary. But I think you need more depth in the subject field to really apply it to those things." Meanwhile, Josh was going into the final year at his old institution and was excited to get going on his dissertation. He understood it to be an important capstone to his degree and made clear that he would approach it in a genuinely interdisciplinary way, rather than "clumsily shoehorn[ing]" it in as others might. Josh made humorous reference to what I am calling 'hyper-interdisciplinarity' as 'cult-like' throughout and considered it important to have people who were not true believers around to cut through the potential groupthink: "Thinking about it now, it's almost better that you have people telling you that it's bullshit along the way, to stop yourself from going head over heels for it sometimes."

Asif, who, as we have seen, doubted the capacity of applied, core modules to achieve intellectual depth, self-deprecatingly and tellingly recounted his "confusion" about the meaning of interdisciplinarity itself:

> 'And I still am kind of confused after two years and my year abroad about what [interdisciplinarity] really means. They can give you the definition as, like, you know, "You're using two different disciplines to synthesise new material that you wouldn't have got [otherwise]." But I remember from my first assessment, I was talking about how, like – using satellite data as well as anthropological data to date the movement of the first people into North America. Something like that. And I remember the teacher telling me, "That's all just archaeology. That's all just modern archaeology."'

In one sense, this argument is similar to Konstantina's point much earlier in this chapter that disciplines are doing similar sorts of work and that the divisions between them are therefore meaningless. However, in the context of Asif's humorously recounted 'confusion', a different reading is that disciplines are indeed complex and multifaceted, and that rather than this leading us to cast them as useless, we might instead put a sceptical eye over hyper-interdisciplinarity's claims to supersede disciplinary work.

Conclusion

This chapter has sought to disentangle two conceptualisations of interdisciplinarity that often go hand in hand on institutions' promotional websites. The first is routine interdisciplinarity; for instance, where disciplinary specialists work together on research questions, taking it that the most complete account of a problem entails looking at it from as many angles as possible. By contrast, hyper-interdisciplinarity is a critique of disciplines themselves, often taking a highly positivist view that the disciplines are artificial barriers impeding access to the real world. While students sometimes made immoderate claims of this sort in interviews, they more often offered gentle, and often humorous, critiques of hyper-interdisciplinarity, seeking to disentangle it from those aspects of interdisciplinarity they valued highly.

As throughout this book, students' complex, plural and questioning accounts often move us beyond the celebratory entanglements of institutions' promotional websites. While institutions may present market values of choice as all that students want, or make hyperbolic claims about the liberal arts saving the world, students themselves are rather more circumspect. In Chapter 3, we will see students' highly plural and complex accounts again in the context of qualities that are often said to be fostered by the applied core modules explored in this chapter: generic skills like team work, communication and lateral thinking.

3

Distinctly indistinct: generic skills and the unique student

Humanities degrees as unique as you are. (Website, private)

In this chapter, I address myself to the educational knot of the general and the particular for those who promote, teach on and study the liberal arts. Liberal arts degrees are presented on institutions' promotional websites as fostering highly generic skills irrespective of the disciplines taken (as we saw in Chapter 2); yet, there is simultaneously a constant stress that liberal arts students are unique by virtue of the specific degree they study.

The desire to forge one's own path through education, work and, more broadly, interests and style can take on a decidedly moral character. As Boltanski and Chiapello (2005: 504) note, there is a growing moral imperative to seek 'autonomy, spontaneity, authenticity, self-fulfilment, creativity, life' through work and other means, and one consequence in education is a moral stance against off-the-peg degrees. As Burke and McManus (2011) found in their study of art school admission interviews, some ill-defined 'quirkiness' easily becomes prized in this context.

Yet, this individualisation of learning choices happens alongside a homogenisation of the desired outcomes for all learners, irrespective of degree content. Generic personal competences are what should be fostered, such as lateral thinking, communication skills and the universally required capacity to 'work well alone or as part of a team'. These are industrial values for the well-functioning workplace and quite distinct from inspirational ones about following one's personal passions.

Values that appear at first sight to be in contradiction, however, may in fact relate to similar processes: *because* the competences are generic and education as a generalised process (learning to learn) is being unmoored from disciplinary specificity, choices about *what* to learn are considered less important. Thus, they can fairly harmlessly be made by students themselves. This highly individualising approach is learner centred (European Commission, 2008) – part of what Gert Biesta (2010) calls 'learnification' – yet, it paradoxically diminishes the importance of the learner's choices. It might be summarised as 'many routes to one destination'.

This relatively recent notion of generic competences, concerned with an efficient workplace, seems entirely divorced again from a much older set of values about general education: the English educational tradition of breadth, generalism and even suspicion of expertise (Young, 2008). We might think here of politics, philosophy and economics degrees, or of the non-specialist, Oxbridge-educated Whitehall civil servant (Mangset, 2015). In fact, my interest in new liberal arts degrees was first piqued by Anthony Grayling's approach to his private, liberal arts-inspired New College of the Humanities and, in particular, the following interview in the *Financial Times*:

> 'To be informed and to be attentive, that's what it is to be a good conversationalist and therefore a good guest at a dinner party,' he says. 'If you could send your graduates out into the world informed and attentive … then you would have really done something valuable for them.' (Warrell, 2015)

This summons a clear-enough picture of the type of character to be developed by a liberal arts education. In Chapter 6, I deal at some length with what we can call the domestic values of ease and style invoked here, as well as their entanglements with the liberal arts and, of course, with social class. For our purposes in *this* chapter, however, I merely note that this old notion of generalism, seemingly very different from both the generic education praised in the supposed learning society and the individualism of learnification, is in fact complexly entangled with both, and this entanglement creates unexpected oddities.

In their seeking of intellectual challenge, for instance, many students find themselves wishing to pursue their curiosity wherever it leads; the notion of the refined generalist, on the other hand, implies a set stock of knowledge, Matthew Arnold's (1993: 77) 'best that has been thought and known', with which the educated mind should be acquainted. Thus, the *generalist* is directed towards a *particular* stock of knowledge, while the more intellectually driven may have cause to eschew specialisation. This indicates that the relationship between the particular and the general is far from straightforward.

Liberal arts degrees are often presented as particularly well placed to equip students with the skills needed to succeed once in a job. They are also promoted, simultaneously, as helping students to *secure* a job. While these appear to be complementary, if not identical, aims, the market concern with securing a job tends to focus on what makes an individual stand out, and this is in contrast with the idea of highly generic competences supposed to prepare young people for work on a practical level. This tension can again present peculiarities, as when one elite university encourages applicants to refer to the now-defunct general studies and critical thinking A level syllabus as the best preparation for its wide-ranging admissions assessment while, on another page, explaining that 'We do not recognise General Studies and Critical Thinking for admissions purposes' (website, old). While the people who set admissions requirements do not tend to be the same people who write the degree, this is a clear enough example of the ways in which market considerations of a qualification's *perceived* value can be in conflict with industrial ones about what type of education will lead to useful skills.

The distinction between this chapter and the next is that I focus on questions of specialisation here, while in Chapter 4, the questions relate to vocationalism. These clearly connected issues are not the same. A university degree may be specialist without explicitly preparing students for a job (indeed, this is still the standard model in England). It may be vocational without being highly specialist (for instance, the training in biology, biochemistry, demography and psychology that a non-specialist medical student might receive in some systems). Yet, some discussions of liberal arts' travels outside of the North American context can end up conflating these two qualities, thus slipping from the idea that what makes liberal arts degrees unique in the world is their non-specialist character, to the claim that they are the only instances of non-vocational higher education in the world – a particularly bold assertion when framed this starkly. In Mary-Ellen Boyle's (2019: 232) very helpful treatment of global liberal arts, for instance, she notes: 'Although still small in scale compared to specialist and/or professional post-secondary degree programs, global liberal education merits scholarly attention.' This suggests that such degrees are outliers in non-North American contexts because of the strangeness of both non-specialisation and non-vocationalism in equal measure. While acknowledging that there is a clear relationship between these features, I have tried to think them through separately, dedicating this chapter to specialisation and the next to vocationalism.

While institutions' promotional websites tend to blithely entangle these very different sorts of values (the inspirational and the domestic; the industrial and the market) some students, in different ways, try to disentangle them. At times, students doubt whether mutually agreed-upon educational values are being successfully upheld by institutions, while at others, they question, more radically, whether the correct values have been identified at all. Indeed, far from *responding* to calls from students, institutions may use 'what students want' as an explanation for what are in fact institutional decisions.

The chapter begins with a discussion of how the liberal arts fit into a much broader historical shift towards thinking of education as the instillment of generic competences as against specific skills. Much is made on institutional websites, as seen in Chapter 2, of the 'real world' and its relation (or lack of relation) to what goes on in universities. Far from *universities* promoting a love of learning for its own sake to instrumentalist students suspicious of the ivory tower, however, I argue that things often work in the opposite direction.

The chapter then goes on to focus on questions of specialisation and expertise, arguing that while some students suggest a moral relationship between breadth of interests and open-mindedness (a narrower set of interests, conversely, demonstrating narrow-mindedness), for many, the question of specialisation is not *whether* to do it, but rather when. Next, we turn to questions of individuality and the special liberal arts student, again showing how this narrative might be bought into or problematised by students in complex ways. Finally, the chapter reflects on notions of 'standing out' in the crowded job market and how institutions seek to reconcile this promise with the highly generic competences they also seek to promote, by paradoxically emphasising the work that students choose to take up *outside* of their degree requirements.

Knowledge, skills and competences

In this section, I place the emergence of liberal arts degrees in the context of a broader, well-documented set of changes in ideas about education. Specifically, this section examines how we have moved away from a clear separation of knowledge and skills, towards thinking about knowledge and skills together as competences. The section also shows how, contra some common understandings, students' perception of education conceived as competence training is at times ambivalent, if not actually resistant.

'Competence' is a term, borrowed from human resource management literature, that came to prominence as an educational idea in the 1970s. This was in the context of concerns that European nations would fail to compete with other states in the knowledge economy of the future. In these imagined futures, investments in technical knowhow, or abstract know*that*, would not pay dividends because technology and society would move on at such a rate that these specialist skills and knowledges would rapidly become obsolete. Instead, the blending of knowhow and knowthat as competences, marrying skills and knowledge with character traits, attitudes and behaviours, would ensure the emergence of a highly flexible, resilient workforce able to respond at pace to an ever-changing economic and social landscape (Pépin, 2007). Competences are necessarily forward-looking, always ready to be applied to some new situation. They are not, then, merely a measure of past or current performance.

While most forms of higher education in England today promote this idea of competence development at least to some extent, websites promoting liberal arts degrees tend to place the notion front and centre:

> Graduates of Liberal Arts and related programmes are highly employable, not only on account of the knowledge, understanding, and skills which they have acquired in each of their subjects but also, and more fundamentally, because of the broad range of their skills, their adaptability, their capacity to make connections, and their independence of mind. (Website, old)

Competences, such as communication skills, intercultural sensitivity and the ability to be a lifelong learner itself, are transversal, meaning that they are dislodged from any particular context – unlike *skills*, which can only be activated in a specific environment. The ability to solder, for instance, is a skill and dependent on the presence of relevant materials and tools. The ability to be a team player, on the other hand, is carried around by the competent from place to place. We are here, then, in the realms of a trainable personal identity (Ingram and Allen, 2019). While it is a very different context, we might compare liberal arts websites' claims about the type of personality this education will develop in learners to government aims to 'responsibilise' welfare recipients (Cantillon and Van Lancker, 2013): the modern subject in both contexts must be a resilient, adaptable self-starter.

This blurring of the boundary between the educational project and the project of the self (Claus et al, 2018) can similarly be related to a broader idea, both within Europe and beyond, that preparation for the workplace should not be separated from personal and social concerns (Esping-Anderson, 2002). As expressed in a European Commission (1995: 4) white paper: 'in modern Europe the three essential requirements of social integration, the enhancement of employability and personal fulfilment, are not incompatible. They should not be brought into conflict, but should on the contrary be closely linked.' Paradoxically, this is a broadening out so that good preparation for work is simultaneously good preparation for life, at the same time as a narrowing down, so that personal and social concerns are important only as they connect to workplace preparation (Telling and Serapioni, 2019). As we will see in this chapter and Chapter 4, liberal arts degrees are promoted on websites *both* as preparation for work (indeed, often obscuring the very difference between education and work), *and* as facilitating the development of the 'whole person'. General education is here presented as the panacea to a whole range of social ills.

While the focus on generic competences signifies a move away from conceiving of knowledge as a straightforward knowthat, this does not make the liberal arts devoid of content. As we saw in Chapter 2, general education often gets its substance through problem-based learning or, more generally, through application. As we have seen, there is a moral twist often given to this focus on 'the questions that matter' (website, post-war), where relevance and application are contrasted with ivory-tower abstractions: 'Instead of learning for learning's sake, [our students] have the skill and experience to apply their scholarship in a wide variety of settings' (website, old). The point is consistently stressed that the purpose of all this application is precisely to develop the competences required to succeed in the modern workplace: 'we take you out of the lecture hall to work with local organisations on real problems, identifying creative solutions and designing a campaign to deliver them' (website, old).

Claims to mimic the workplace in order to develop transversal competences, however, tend to run up against the problem that education is *something else*. When it comes to assessments, for instance, working in teams has become increasingly prized as an authentic endeavour that will test for the qualities needed in the workplace. The ability to work in a team is considered a key competence that graduates should possess. Programme director Maria explained that this was a key difference between the liberal arts and more conventional humanities degrees on which she had worked at her old institution: "The emphasis is very much right from the word 'go' on communication skills and working with other people."

Students are encouraged to work in teams as if they would not develop any communal or civic spirit otherwise, despite all the ways they demonstrate this spirit outside of assessment: in their informal study groups, hopes for future work in teams and all the communality that characterises student living. Yet, in this instance, they feel keenly the tension between collaborative work as competence development for the workplace and the highly individualist, competitive assessment that remains a mainstay of university education (McArthur, 2011). They will be given a mark out of a hundred for their teamwork, and this mark will be placed against their individual name and used to rank them against their peers.

First-year undergraduate Lotte was a diligent student, enjoying her degree at an old institution and committed to the idea of the liberal arts. Her assessment of this knot of industrial and market values within assessed teamwork was, however, gently critical and repeated by many students:

> 'Everybody really just had to really work together and – How am I going to phrase this? – basically, we were dependent on each other: what the one person wrote was basically a basis for what the other people were going to write, so you were really dependent on each other. That requires quite some teamwork and coordination, and that proved to be fairly challenging not only for my group, but for all the others.'

Like many students who made this point, Lotte's critique is careful and seems to point towards her own weakness as what made the assessment 'challenging'. There is a kind of humility in Lotte suggesting that she does not possess the industrial worth to succeed in such a challenge. However, as Boltanski and Thévenot (2006: 225) note, such acts of self-deprecation are 'first attempts at critiques'. By doubting their own worth, students actually cast doubt on the relevance of industrial values to this particular educational context.

Through examples such as this, I do not mean to suggest that students reject industrial values altogether. As will be shown in Chapter 4, they think a great deal about future employment and its relationship to education. Rather, what students seem to be problematising here are institutions' blithe attempts to smooth over these contradictory entanglements and, in particular, attempts merely to ape the workplace as if education had no purpose beyond the development of generic competences. This runs directly counter to the story that universities are places trying to instil a love of learning in otherwise instrumentally minded students. In examples like this, it is students who buy into the idea of the ivory tower, from which the forward-minded institution feels a need to distance itself in order to get closer to the 'real world'.

Against expertise? Students on specialisation

> The purpose of such breadth is to provide you with the broad-based education and skills to become a leader, not just an expert. (Website, private)

As educational models turn to the development of transversal competences and away from notions of technical or other expertise, university talk appears to disconnect to an extent from concerns with the specific content of degrees (Ashwin, 2020). Degrees can come to be presented as apparatus for instilling generic competences, almost divorced from any consideration of specific knowledge or expertise. As I suggested in the introduction to this chapter, we can think of this as a broadening out of the routes by which one may reach an increasingly narrow set of outcomes. In Niels åkerstrøm Andersen's (2007: 347) words: 'Learning how to learn is disconnected from learning something definite.'

The applicant guidance for an admissions assessment for one liberal arts degree is instructive in this context: 'The markers will be looking for examples of flair, linguistic accuracy and style, the ability to make interesting and relevant connections and links, and the ability to contextualise knowledge where appropriate, so there is nothing specific that you will need to revise before taking the test' (website, old). As one student testimonial on a website also puts it: 'At times I'd get frightened at not knowing the nitty gritty of every revolution such as the dates of every event [etc], but I was reassured that those fact[s] were the least important aspect of the module' (student testimonial, website, post-war). However, in this section, I argue that, despite this framing, many liberal arts students do consider themselves to be content or disciplinary specialists. This is something that seemed to change as they worked their way through their degree.

It's true that the specific content of degrees was sometimes considered less important than other factors, even by students. Having now completed his degree and been through multiple job interviews and assessment centres,

Devendra noted that, from the perspective of employers, "I think degree [subject] matters less now. Classification matters more and more." However, importantly, this is his sense of what it takes to compete on the job market; on a personal level, Devendra had a strong sense of the importance of choosing disciplines that pique your interest and regretted that he had tended to prioritise the former over the latter. In examples like this, students are aware of and care about what has market value, but they do not compound this with more personal concerns.

More hesitantly, students sometimes expressed uncertainty about the value of acute specialisation in the arcana of disciplines. Here, they tended to distinguish between a general interest in disciplines and a more technicist or pedantic fixation on them. Will, who had just finished his degree at a post-war university, had moved over from psychology to the liberal arts early in his course. As he explained: "It wasn't the maths itself. It was getting bogged down in the maths which I didn't enjoy."

In this context, extreme disciplinary expertise was sometimes conceived of as a problematic narrowing, not only of one's future employment options, but also, and connected to this, of one's overall world view. Here, an almost moral view of specialists as narrow-*minded* – potentially even drone-like – is suggested. Second-year student Ellie, like many I talked to at more elite institutions, did not want to work in the private sector. She connected a lack of specialism at the degree level to more varied and fulfilling types of work, and travelled from there to a moral conception of her being in the world:

'You're not blinkered: you kind of have quite a, like, large overall view of the world, rather than just kind of a narrow focus on one discipline. And I think because of that, because of that way of thinking and that kind of understanding of how the world works, I can't imagine myself going into a job in the private sector, where I was just doing the same thing all the time and kind of just wasn't having that wider outlook on how what I'm doing is impacting on the world, I guess.'

Here, Ellie weaves between quite different ideas: beginning with a discussion of interdisciplinarity and its relationship to her overall world view, she goes on to discuss her ideal future work, which is outside the private sector, socially beneficial and varied. While there is a link between the first two aspects, how this relates to the work's level of monotony is unclear.

It is not only more academically or scientifically minded individuals who are at risk of narrow-mindedness or pedantry. Konstantina, a second-year student at an old university who had chosen the liberal arts over creative arts with some difficulty, noted that friends of hers who studied only the latter felt unable to keep up when conversation turned to "politics and life and books".

Ellie's moral way of thinking about her ideal, wide-ranging future work is generally regarded as an academically legitimate way of thinking; that is, it is not likely to be received as careerism (Hurst, 2013). Yet, we could argue that hoping one's job will fill all kinds of social and personal needs is *more* careerist (in the sense of career-centred) than merely wanting a job to get rich.

While we might expect most students who choose the liberal arts to feel this way about specialisation, though, there is in fact a great deal of variety. Just as institutions themselves may approach degree structure in more or less individualist or prescriptive ways, so students express different preferences, and many of those towards the end of their degrees *did* think of themselves as specialists, rather than generalists. Some stressed the importance of degree coherence or an intellectual thread (or, in hindsight, regretted its absence), and this thread was sometimes related to the desire for a challenging syllabus that ran throughout my interviews with students. Over time, dilettantish ideas about becoming Grayling's 'refined generalist' from the introduction to this chapter were replaced with notions of rigour. Josh, for instance, had just come back to his old institution after spending his third year in the US. He compared the more structured, and progressively more difficult, curriculum at his English institution to the relative free-for-all he had experienced there:

> 'I think I prefer doing a lot of really, really hard modules across the board within a more structured sort of thing than doing loads of modules that I don't really find that challenging but give you a good skillset in everything. There's advantages of this – advantages to both I think.'

This desire for expertise was also present in some students' reservations about the wide-ranging and intellectually fragmented nature of core modules, related to concerns about the inherent shallowness of pre-disciplinary interdisciplinarity itself (Barrett, 2012). In this context, however, reference was often made to final assessments as where complexity *would* be developed – crucially, not assessments that asked students to draw from across the curriculum or work in interdisciplinary teams, but rather those that allowed them to select and *specialise* in just one of the disparate topics covered. As second-year student Ben, studying at a post-war institution, explained:

> 'It would be a different thinker every week. So, we'd only really get time to understand that author at an introductory level. What I have enjoyed, having said that, is – the essays that I've enjoyed the most have been when I clearly enjoyed a lecture or a seminar, and I like the ideas that a certain thinker is putting forward, and then I go and do my own research on them.'

This is one example of a broader pattern, then, where specialisation was seen as what followed after, rather than being replaced by, general education.

Second-year student Konstantina was just coming to a sense of what she most wanted to study on her very wide-ranging degree at an old university, and she expressed the sentiments of many students clearly: "I mean, I don't think we shouldn't specialise. I just think we should all start with a wider variety of options and then specialise as we go on." She had recently considered transferring out from the liberal arts into her preferred discipline, along with friends who had felt, "Oh, it's bullshit. We're not specialising." However, she remained philosophical about staying with the liberal arts, believing that she could only have come to discover her preference for one discipline by studying a range of them at university level.

Science specialist Victoria was now in her second year at an old institution and beginning to think seriously about future options. For her, the desire to continue to specialise meant developing expertise through postgraduate work: "So, after my degree, I definitely want to go on and do a master's because I'd like to be able to say, 'Yes, I did this kind of broad and weird undergraduate degree, but then I did something, and I chose it.'" Of course, any educational trajectory will probably move from the general to the particular; what often characterises liberal arts students is a resistance to the precise type of specialisation at the precise transition point most common in England. This is unlike the idea that students should not be specialising at all given the future's fundamental unknowability, often promoted, as we will see in Chapter 4, on institutions' websites. Instead, many students present a preference for specialisation but *after* a prolonged period of experimentation has taken place.

It would be tempting to understand this deferral of specialisation in the broader context of massification: as more students enter higher education and, in turn, more progress to postgraduate study (Marvell, 2021), the dividing lines between general education and specialisation begin to shift. Indeed, the prevalence of the liberal arts model in the US has been connected, by some, to a relatively high proportion of the population accessing some form of higher education. This supposedly means that the attainment of the school leaving certificate signifies a lower level of general education in comparison to some European counterparts, as that level can be topped up in the first two years of higher education (see, for example, van der Wende, 2017).

Institutions' promotional websites might explicitly appeal to applicants by suggesting that liberal arts degrees facilitate a less jarring transition to university, precisely by more closely mirroring the school curriculum than disciplinary degrees: 'You have spent your time in school and college having a broad education, studying different subjects and we want to continue and expand that at university' (website, old). As one student testimonial on a website makes clear, this might extend beyond academic considerations, to a conception of the liberal arts cohort, and community, as remaining closer to the school experience:

> Socially, since each year group of Liberal Arts students is between twenty and thirty people, you will have a base of likeminded peers who you will become incredibly close to, but will be able to be a part of larger lectures and other small seminar groups through your major subject which I think makes the step up from sixth-form to university education much less daunting. (Student testimonial, website, old)

There are two important caveats to make to the purported connection between general education and massification, however. First, in some, more elite English contexts, the notion of general education for undergraduates is not in fact new. Oxford's philosophy, politics and economics degree, for instance, has enjoyed a long history preparing the next generation of politicians, civil servants and other elite professionals (Scott, 2002). And more broadly than this, the notion of a humanities or arts education preceding professional training is not new in wealthier spheres. For Lijuan, now in her third year at an old institution, whose parents in China remained unconvinced of the value of a liberal arts education, this elite tradition could be invoked as a kind of reassurance:

> 'My guardian was saying, "Before the age of 24 you should let them do whatever they like, because it doesn't really matter." 'Cause her daughter, like, did music for university and then did a one-year law conversion, and now she's a lawyer. So, it doesn't really matter. And her son did linguistics and then went into banking, that sort of stuff. So!'

The second point to make here is that while it may make sense to connect the expansion of general education at university level to massification, we should be wary about moving from this observation to a critical argument that young people are forever expanding their childhoods and seeking infantilisation through education. Such a view relies on a historically contingent take on the life course as marked by specific milestones that must be reached by a certain age, what Henry Blatterer (2007: 3) calls 'standard adulthood'. Looking at youth transitions in this normative way reifies the conception of adulthood developed during a specific period – the post-war era – as a universal definition. The problem with this approach will be explored further in Chapter 4.

A course for individuals: on being different

'Everyone in my degree is a bit crazy in their own way.' (Konstantina, second-year student, old)

As we have seen, the relationship between the general and the particular is extremely complex in the context of liberal arts degrees. As we have also seen, some students take a different view from that presented on institutional websites. For instance, rather than eschewing specialist expertise altogether, students towards the end of their degree tended to view themselves as disciplinary experts who had come to their particular interest late, rather than not at all. In this section, we return to the idea that while the competences thought to be instilled by the liberal arts are highly generic (and thus the same for all students on such courses), the routes to these general competences are highly disparate. This relates to the idea that liberal arts students are fundamentally *individuals* and thus require a bespoke degree that allows them to express that individuality. However, while this notion from promotional websites was to an extent reinforced by relatively privileged students, a number of others sought to criticise such ideas about the special liberal arts student – sometimes inflecting that critique with a classed analysis.

There are a number of ways that liberal arts degrees are conceived of, both on websites and by some students, as particularly suiting 'individuals'. First, and most obviously, there is the bespoke nature of the degree structure itself and how such flexibility is promoted as in keeping with an individualist logic: 'Every liberal arts degree is unique to each individual student' (website, old).

Then, there are ideas about the specialness of the liberal arts cohort and faculty as a whole due to the degree's innovative aspects. Liberal arts students are thus simultaneously conceived of as a group of unique *individuals* and as a unique *group* of individuals. In the latter case, notions of cohort identity are strong: 'You'll form a community of ambitious, focused and forward-looking students, who are keen to chart their own path through education and who, like you, share the qualities of open-mindedness, alertness and maturity' (website, post-war).

Liberal arts student Agathe spoke to me while studying abroad for her third year and contrasted her English post-war university's fostering of this cohort identity with the more cold and formulaic approach of her host institution. She characterised her own university's highly personalised approach as, "You've chosen us and we've chosen you." Thus, students are framed as individuals who nonetheless share key qualities. As a number of students maintained, what unites liberal arts students may actually be individuality itself. Second-year student Mathilde noted this paradox when she observed that at her old institution, "it is very diverse, but they all stand out in the crowd, if that makes sense?"

Connected to notions of the special degree, in some places, there is an emphasis on one individual as the charismatic lynchpin of the course. As well as being invoked through student testimonials on websites, some student interviewees flagged an individual lecturer as integral to the degree's success. Now in her final year, Phoebe still remembered meeting a particularly charming academic for the first time and the impact this had on her choice of a post-war university: "He was quite fantastic. Very eccentric but a fantastic guy, and I met him on the open day and he was very charismatic." However, other students, as we will see, expressed some reservations about this emphasis placed on individual lecturers.

The moral character of the injunction to individuality was implied in interviews by students with some hesitancy. A criticism of those who are less clearly 'individuals' was implied yet simultaneously disavowed, as when third-year student Asif evocatively described students on other degrees at his old institution:

'Obviously, no disrespect to people on other courses, who also – I've met some really interesting students from other courses, but sometimes you're in a business class, and there's a guy from accounting, and you never met a more accounting guy in your life. He does Excel for fun. Or, you're in a physics class, and, again, I've seen people that look – I'd forgotten people could be like that. It's like an American high-school terrible film stereotype.'

In a less jocular way, third-year student Josh also alluded with some hesitancy towards the individuality of liberal arts students as compared to others: "I don't think anyone thinks that they're better than other people, but I think people know that – they feel different from the rest of the people at [the university] in some ways." This belief seemed to be particularly pronounced at the old university that both Asif and Josh attended, where students perceived the degree to be something of a favourite of senior management. The sense was that "a massive amount of funding" had been allocated, eventually being spent on "random stuff like avocado sandwiches", as Asif put it.

Often, students related notions of individuality to intelligence. Many reported that school had been easy, though whether this led to a sense of specialness depended on a range of factors, including family and school context. First-year student Lotte's mother had become concerned very early in her daughter's school career that she was not being challenged and intervened in order to get extra work from the school to develop her talents. Meanwhile, fourth-year student Phoebe described her comprehensive school as one where no one noticed or pushed pupils unless they were within a specific, middle range of attainment, currently failing but with hopes they could be pushed up to a pass (see Marks, 2014).

As 'good' students, there was sometimes conflict between what the school expected (that they would pursue the most prestigious subjects if they had an aptitude for them) and the students' own, more curiosity-led approach. While following the most prestigious path seemed obvious to teachers, students, on the other hand, felt a tension between these values. Second-year student Mathilde felt significant pressure from the school to follow in her parents' footsteps as doctors but was clear that she wanted to pursue the humanities and social sciences when she got to her elite university: "My teachers, I think, advised me to continue in maths, biology, physics. Because I was very good at it, and that's what's privileged in France to study. If you are good at it, you should study that. I don't know: it's a weird approach!" Where students had rejected the most prestigious routes in order to pursue the liberal arts, the school's bafflement could be particularly pronounced: when comprehensive student Jessica turned down an offer to study at Cambridge in order to take the liberal arts at a less prestigious (though certainly elite) institution, she had "had teachers come up to me and sort of tell me that I was crazy to my face".

For those from very elite backgrounds, where transition into the most prestigious universities was not perceived as particularly remarkable, the decision to study the liberal arts was contrasted with the relatively frictionless and time-honoured progression expected by the school. Asif (third-year student, old), who had attended one of the most elite public schools in the country, related in a strikingly offhand manner the easiest option that had been available to him: "I was basically going to apply to Oxford for geography just because I didn't know what else to do. Because I was just like, 'I'm good at this. This is kind of what people do from my school. I guess I'll just do this.'"

The perception of individual specialness is different for these students. Asif, who was not regarded as particularly special in the context of his school, suggested his specialness in relation to the stereotypical normality of students studying regular disciplines. The bespoke nature of his course allowed him to express this difference. For many other, less privileged students, school *had* been a place where specialness was noted, and the decision to pursue an unconventional degree was regarded as a waste of this talent. Yet, in both sorts of cases, there is a link made between specialness and polymathy, where the ability to move between subjects with some ease was believed by students to convey talent (Mangset, 2015). Asif, again, suggested this link when describing other students at his liberal arts assessment day: "The people I met and stuff, I was like, 'Yeah, these guys and girls are so smart. They seem to know about everything.'"

The students here appear to match institutions' ideas about the ideal liberal arts candidate with complex and plural motivations: ambitious yet reflexive;

open-minded yet wilful; intellectually motivated and highly able, yet with a concern for the ultimate 'point' of their studies. By contrast, the non-ideal liberal arts student is conceived, at least by some senior academics, as just an indecisive one. Former dean Larry described the different sorts of students that had tended to come to open days when he had been involved in the liberal arts at his institution. In distinction to the ideal, complex student outlined earlier, "The other kind of student that gets attracted to liberal arts is the kind of student that can't make up their mind what they want to do and think, 'Oh, this is a programme that lets me do anything.' And they're probably going to be disappointed." As Sara Ahmed (2015) has pointed out, academics can be inclined to decry student instrumentalism when what students want is different from what academics themselves want.

A number of students, however, expressed their reservations about the assumed links between intelligence, polymathy and individuality. Jessica and Josh attended the same old institution and told more complicated stories, both about their own specialness and about the aura of uniqueness surrounding their degrees. State-educated finalist Jessica expressed concern that her fellow, largely privately educated students appeared to regard themselves as "very, very special", suspecting that this might relate to their class backgrounds. She also questioned the inherent link between polymathy and intelligence, asserting that, "I'm not as good at maths as lots of people who did maths [only], and I'm nowhere near as good at English as lots of people who did English."

Having previously noted the relative ease with which he had moved between academic subjects at school, third-year student Josh went on to question whether the correct way to think about this was as intelligence: "I think growing up, I probably thought that I was just smart, but in reality, I don't think I was particularly smarter than other kids. I think I was just more adept at flitting from subject to subject." Like Jessica, he also went beyond this kind of self-critique, to question the culture of uniqueness that the degree fostered (in particular, when it came to the focus on individual, charismatic lecturers):

> 'I think there's times when you'd see a crowd of 20 people around one man, everyone's wide-eyed and hung on his every word, that you're a bit like, "Hmm, this is a weird set-up for an academic environment." It seems almost like he's giving a Sermon on the Mount sort of thing. … It's kind of nice but a little sinister from time to time.'

As programme director Hélène pointed out, these individualist notions of the brilliant professor, repeated in student testimonials on websites and in some of my own interviews with students, tend to repeat familiar scripts about gender, ethnicity, nationality and age. Hélène went so far as to connect the degree's difficulties with recruitment at her post-war university to the fact that "it looks like a bit of a single-person operation. And the single person was me: a foreign woman."[1]

While institutional websites tend to stress student, lecturer, cohort, degree and institutional uniqueness as unmitigated goods, then, some of the people engaged in liberal arts endeavours remain at least ambivalent. Moreover, even when notions of specialness are embraced, we should be wary of conflating this individualist, inspirational mode too simplistically with market-driven consumerism. There are affinities, but while an inspirational desire to express oneself through education is inflected with individual passion and desire, this is very different from a rationalist consumerism concerned with bang–buck equivalence. Indeed, a market rationality relies on notions of similar desires from similarly placed consumers (Boltanski and Thévenot, 2006), which is quite different from students' concerns that their individuality be recognised.

Stand out: selling yourself on the job market

In this final section, we turn to how institutions' promotional websites conceptualise the graduate labour market. Here, the industrial concern with preparation for actually being in a job (that is, the focus we see elsewhere on competences) is completely superseded by a market concern with *acquiring* a job only. And while the idea of generic competences as the best preparation for the job market suggests that the specific content of a degree matters less and less, the liberal arts are actually sold here on the premise that they allow their graduates to *stand out* on the crowded job market. Here, it turns out that what will get the liberal arts graduate a job has nothing to do with either generic skills *or* with degree content, but rather concerns the extra-curricular pursuits students take up outside of their course.

Echoing Michael Tomlinson's (2008) student participants' refrain that 'the degree is not enough', liberal arts degrees are marketed as providing that extra something to ensure visibility on the labour market, a claim sometimes explicitly related to massification and the supposed problem of 'too many graduates'. This might get connected to some elusive general market value that liberal arts degrees are purported to hold, perhaps because of the unusualness of the degree itself: 'With more people going to university now than ever before, it is not necessarily enough to just have a degree and know you'll get a job. Employers have the pick of hundreds of people per

---

[1] When students did talk about senior female academics, they tended to be positioned as intimidating, rather than inspiring. As third-year student Agathe remarked about one senior staff member at her post-war institution, "She's a very strong woman, and I feel very afraid of her."

position and so you'll need to stand out – and [our] students do' (student testimonial, website, old).

However, while the visibility of liberal arts graduates is sometimes related to skills or to some general sense of unusualness, it is often connected to extra-curricular activities, placements and study abroad (that is, to aspects of the student experience that are supplementary to degree content). Work placements are sometimes promoted as a necessity, even when they are not embedded within a course; rather, the degree is thought to instil a kind of thoughtful proactivity in this direction:

> I'm grateful for so many things I experienced during university, but one of them is the ambition that the core modules instilled in me, often emphasising how important it is to supplement your time at university with internships and networking. Many people don't realise these things until the end of their degree, when it's too late. (Student testimonial, website, old)

Here, it is suggested that the degree itself will create an appetite for career-boosting extra-curricular pursuits. This is despite the fact that the general narrative of student specialness implies that the liberal arts-minded applicant *already has* such qualities of proactivity and extra-curricular chutzpah: '[liberal arts] students are, by nature, dynamic, busy people with lots of interests both within and outside the classroom' (website, old). Indeed, many of the students I talked to related that they had pursued a wide range of both academic and extra-academic interests since school. Second-year student Marta remarked that many of her liberal arts peers at her old institution had, like her, pursued a range of interests, hobbies and clubs since school and into university:

> 'I think [liberal arts] people do tend to like to get involved in lots of things. Again, I don't know if it's something that can be generalised, but from people that I know, everybody seems to be involved in at least one other, or a few other things outside of their studies.' (Marta, second-year student, old)

Yet, institutions often piggyback on such pursuits *as if they reflected something about the education provided*: 'Employers recognise the value of a degree from a university with an international reputation for academic excellence, and of the wide range of skills which our students develop through their extensive involvement in sport, theatre, music, community service and many other activities' (website, old). Such a claim has little to say about degree content; instead, it stresses what is learned through extra-curricular interests – interests that many liberal arts students have before attending university anyway.

Indeed, the pushing of extra-curricular pursuits, especially at elite universities, can become so acute that one begins to wonder why it's worth bothering with the degree at all. The following example is only the more absurd end of an almost universal promotional website genre: the Very Keen Student Testimonial:

> I joined the music society, was part of the group who founded the [liberal arts] society, worked as a waitress at uni, joined the sailing club on my year abroad (I couldn't sail at all at the time), gained an internship with a professional Australian orchestra, managed my host university's orchestral tour to China when abroad, played club hockey, was a student ambassador and student representative, and gained an internship bursary from the university. In my [job] interviews, most of the time was spent talking about these experiences, the skills I gained from them and how they could help within a new job. (Student testimonial, website, old)

The Very Keen Student Testimonial is presumably included on liberal arts websites because it says something about the opportunities available to applicants to this particular degree at this particular university. Yet, because it says nothing unique about the university (and nothing about the degree *at all*), the reader is left instead with an impression of this particular student and their remarkable energy levels. Indeed, were every student to take up extra-curricular opportunities at this alarming rate, each one would singularly *fail* to stand out (and we would need a lot more hockey teams). And while part-time jobs and (some) student societies are relatively universal opportunities (thus offering little value on the job market), you don't have to be Pierre Bourdieu to notice that study abroad, sailing clubs and orchestral tours of China are a rather different prospect.

While academics may seek to mitigate the effects of some students' privilege when accessing extra-curricular opportunities, they are of course limited in what they can do. I talked to academics involved in placement modules at an old and a modern university, where embedding such activities into the degree may be expected to even out access to opportunities of this sort. However, these apparently similar modules in fact offered notably different sorts of placements. While teaching fellow Kate at the old university had examples of students working at a film company and a concert hall, programme director Michael described posts at a local records office and a brewery that were available to students at his modern university. Despite concerted efforts from academics, then, the likelihood that different extra-curricular opportunities will exacerbate pre-existing inequalities (for instance, experiences one can draw upon in the Universities and Colleges Admissions Service personal statement [Jones, 2015]) is significant.

This focus on elements outside of degree content contributes to a narrative of university study as a process of self-development that has its end point in the job interview (Brown and Hesketh, 2004). The focus on market worth leaves aside the question of whether sailing or hockey really do impart the skills required in the modern workplace once the job has been secured. It also allows more privileged students at more elite universities to demonstrate an ability to *detach* themselves from 'merely' educational concerns, just as elite students in Pierre Bourdieu's (1996) *State Nobility* pursued interests that were not (yet) consecrated by the school, such as film or jazz, or, more recently, Ciaran Burke's (2016) middle-class participants downplayed the role of the school when discussing their achievements. For less privileged students, or for those for whom opportunities are different, the relentless 'degree is not enough' narrative can be unhelpful and exclusionary.

Conclusion

The relationship between the general and the particular throws up a range of complicated tensions for those who promote, teach on and study liberal arts degrees. While the much broader educational shift towards generic and transversal competences discourages specialisation, some students are uncertain of the value of this move, sometimes regarding themselves as specialists and often making explicit calls for intellectual rigour and depth within their education. And while a narrative of individuality and specialness is consistently evoked by institutions hoping to appeal to what is imagined to be a highly individualist cohort, students themselves are again sometimes resistant to this appeal, placing themselves within the realms of the normal.

We can understand these tensions by thinking about the complex, plural values at play in English higher education today. Notions of the broadly informed generalist as what (elite) English education should produce are as old as the hills (Young, 2008) and relate to domestic values of authority, charisma and 'civility' (Rothblatt, 1976). When reference is made to what it means to be a good dinner-party guest, or when breadth is contrasted with pedantry, such a value system is invoked. This domestic idea prizes a kind of understated and general wisdom that is quite at odds with inspirational values of almost manic intellectual curiosity; yet, we see a compromise between these values when generic personal attributes like resilience and cultural sensitivity are said to be imparted through the pursuit of one's individual intellectual desires.

Meanwhile, market and industrial values appear to be more aligned given that, in this context, both often relate to future work. However, while market considerations relate to the ways that liberal arts students may stand out as *individuals* on the job market, industrial values relate to *generic* competences said to be needed once workers are in post. As we have just seen, institutions' promotional websites stress market values when it comes to the relationship between the liberal arts and work, and rarely stress generic competences here. As we will see in Chapter 4, however, students themselves remain deeply concerned that they should be well prepared for *work*, rather than merely for a job interview.

4

Jobs for the generalist: non-vocational degrees and employability

New liberal arts degrees are particularly sold on the generic skills they impart (as we saw in Chapter 3) and, in particular, the idea that through them, one 'learns to learn'. The idea is that, as opposed to the specific content imparted through disciplinary degrees, what is needed today is the ability to move quickly between projects and apply existing knowledge in new settings: adaptability, flexibility and a capacity for lateral thinking. Liberal arts are, then, thought of as an especially good training for the current job market, and liberal arts graduates are thought of as particularly employable.

It is difficult to amass meaningful evidence to show that liberal arts graduates have strong employment outcomes because so few students take them in any one national system, exacerbating the problems of controlling for institution and class effects, among other factors (Godwin, 2015a). In the English context, liberal arts degrees tend to be grouped under 'combined honours' for national statistical purposes. This is a very broad umbrella category that includes most degrees taken at the Open University, the largest higher education provider in the UK by number of students, with a strong remit for widening participation. As such, it is difficult to get a picture of graduate outcomes for the liberal arts at a national level, though the introduction of a 'liberal arts' code under the new Higher Education Classification of Subjects should make these easier to track, as well as indicating the term's increasing recognisability. While it is possible to compare outcomes for each individual degree against the average for that institution, the small numbers as well as the lack of demographic data at that level would make such comparisons unhelpful.

Therefore, instead of focusing on whether liberal arts graduates 'are' particularly employable, here, I explore *narratives* of employability as they are told on universities' promotional webpages, as well as how such stories are complicated by some students and staff – especially those at modern universities, or who are in some ways less privileged than others. They are critical of attempts to present just one sort of educational value (for instance, an industrial one about skills or a market one about visibility on the job market) as the truth of the liberal arts. Nor do they conflate them; rather, they seek to interrogate the appropriateness of this or that value in *specific* educational settings.

The chapter begins with a consideration of the familiar idea of work as the 'real world'. Old and post-war universities' websites tend to stress a kind of hard-headed industrial reality when they speak of work as 'the real world' (as if employment constituted the entirety of our experienced reality and education none of it). They tend to promote liberal arts degrees as the best preparation for work because they seemingly mimic that work (through, as we saw in Chapter 2, real-world assessment and the like). However, students refute the simplicity of this picture in different ways.

While they challenge simplistic industrial values here, in the next section, I show how students also refute simplistic market values, through a discussion of the *name* of the degree. This is perceived as a particular problem in terms of the market worth of the course. Students use different strategies to maximise their chances of standing out on the job market, seeking to work around the fact that the liberal arts are still largely an unknown quantity among employers. The fact that students choose the degree despite such difficulties shows us, again, that to focus on the market alone can blind us to the different values at play. Students do not merely wish to 'get a job', but also want to be *well prepared for the future*.

The remainder of the chapter engages with notions of the 'unknown future', of uncertainty and risk, which are central to how universities sell the timeliness of the liberal arts, especially in relation to the job market. While institutional websites promote a very concrete notion of work as the real world, they *simultaneously* present in much less grounded terms what this reality will actually look like once today's students get there. The future is unknowable; thus, a good preparation for it is in fact an acceptance of unknowability and flux. While the contrast here between the concrete and abstract conceptualisations of work goes unremarked on institutions' websites, some students seek to draw attention to it. For instance, first-generation students and those with less financial security may seek to firm up the unknown future by creating certainty, stressing the value of long-term employment over piecemeal projects, or the importance of precise career planning.

To dismiss the desire for enduring, meaningful (and reasonably well-remunerated) work as cynical careerism is all very well when I have enduring, meaningful (and reasonably well-remunerated) work myself. I'm put in mind of a student of mine for whom leaving university to enter low-paid but worthy work made no sense given the sacrifices her parents had faced to get her to that point. To decry her concerns as careerism (especially when 'wanting to change the world' is not) is to close one's eyes to class (Hurst, 2013). Careerism and idealism are not two ends of a scale, so that students who are 'more careerist' are 'less idealist'; rather, these are qualitatively different values, and we may well encounter highly idealist careerists (as in some notions of public office), or indeed cynics without much careerist drive at all. However they think about the future world of work, though, for the vast majority of students, 'education and employment are closely related, and a failure to provide the latter limits what can be achieved by the former' (Ainley, 2016a: 96).

Getting ready for the real world

As we saw in Chapter 2, the movement towards interdisciplinary regions of study, as opposed to discrete, singular subjects, often hangs on a hyper-interdisciplinary belief that the disciplines obstruct access to the real world. Specifically, it suggests a pointing outward towards the economy and away from 'purely' academic concerns (Bernstein, 1996). This is what Mangez and Vanden Broeck (2020) suggest when noting that education now *inhabits* the paradox of 'real-world learning', rather than making a pure claim for education's value in and of itself. This is not to say that such inspirational claims are no longer made by institutions at all, but rather that it is increasingly difficult to make such a purely educational claim without any recourse to extra-educational worth.

While we should note that they refer specifically to an employability module, the following learning outcomes are striking:

> To gain experiences of a real-world consultancy project, working as a team with peers.
>
> To gain experience of producing a team-written, real world consultancy report.
>
> To gain skills relevant to working in the knowledge economy.
> (Website, old)

There is nothing here that alludes to anything beyond the world of work. We don't merely see the linking of learning outcomes to work (logical enough on an employability module), but also the loss of any distinct meaning for 'learning' beyond work experience.

In distinction to this presentation of liberal arts degrees as closer to the real world than other types of education, some students, for different reasons, remain sceptical. As I argue here (and see also Chapter 5), students have a real concern that their course be academically challenging and in different ways reject the values of instrumentalism and careerism that are often attributed to them (and to which they may subscribe, albeit ambivalently, in different contexts).

For Devendra, now finishing his degree at an old university, the claims made to produce work-ready graduates did not match his experience. Describing himself as from a British Indian background where both the sciences and professional vocations were prized, he compared himself to other liberal arts students who focused on the humanities rather than taking up the opportunity to be genuinely interdisciplinary, and seemed to have no clear career aspirations. He did not challenge the placing of industrial values within the educational setting, but rather the extent to which work-relevant competences *were* in fact instilled in the liberal arts model he experienced:

> 'So, [employers] are asking, or want, certain skills from our graduates that they want to employ, but beyond group work, I would say that they haven't really done much. For example, I think in [this university], only 30 per cent of the students have done any science of any kind. So, I'd say most aren't very good with numbers, for example, which I think most employers would definitely be after. I feel like – like I said, it can be very easy to have an easy ride and not push yourself or actually try and do more than one thing. I know people that have only done English and the core modules throughout the degree. So, to me, it doesn't make a huge amount of sense.'

Devendra points towards the knot involving 'pick and mix' and more prescriptive notions of the curriculum. On the one hand, liberal arts degrees promote a highly individualised conception of the curriculum in which students are free to follow their interests. Certainly, most websites try to appeal in this way to prospective applicants. On the other hand, as Devendra points out, the degrees are presented as preparing students for the job market. However, there are in fact two quite different markets here: the market of potential applicants choosing a degree; and the market of potential employers choosing a worker. Far from seamlessly aligning, Devendra notes that the appealing flexibility of the degree is what *stops* liberal arts students from being highly employable, as it gets in the way of them developing the skills, or industrial worth, required. He takes what Bruce Kimball (1986) calls a cultural (as opposed to an individualist) view of general education: there are just some things that educated people should know, and educational consumerism should not impede this.

Here, Devendra challenges the institution on its own terms: yes, education should prepare us for work; no, it doesn't do that. He *tests* the adequacy of the institution according to the values it espouses and finds it wanting. He offers a corrective critique (Holmqvist, 2022) to show how it may more successfully live up to its own values, which Devendra shares.

While Devendra is talking about curricular decisions here, it is perhaps in the domain of assessment that the positive relationship between the liberal arts and the 'real world' of work is most keenly stressed. Liberal arts degrees are promoted as moving education beyond traditional, stuffy and detached modes of assessment, and bringing universities to the real world. Presentations, portfolios and reports are promoted, not because (or at least not only because) they allow the assessment of relevant knowledge, but because mimicking the world of work is taken to be the best preparation for it: 'As your future career won't be essays and exams we encourage you to apply what you learn with assessments that reflect real jobs' (website, old).

When discussing assessment, Asif took his critique a step further than Devendra. Now going into his final year at an old institution, he was not convinced that industrial concerns about the job market and the development of outward-facing, extra-educational competences should, in fact, take prominence in the educational setting, especially when it comes to assessment:

> 'I'll be honest, the assessment was really weird: making podcast talk shows in groups. And I think it was – it was fun as well, but, you know, you get to uni and all your teachers have been like, "Uni's hard." Like, "A levels are like rote learning; uni's hard." And then you're there making a podcast on your phone, or you're answering quiz multiple-choice questions, and you're like, "Is this university? Because I could get used to this."'

"I'll be honest" – Asif is raising our discussion to a consideration of reality, to a radical critique or a dispute (Boltanski and Thévenot, 2006). Similarly, final-year student Lijuan discussed her unhappiness with the use of presentations as a form of assessment at her old institution ("Even in physics!"), noting that while this may be helpful for employability, "those things should be separate to the aims". While the 'real-world' industrial narrative is accepted by Devendra, Asif and Lijuan want to foreground a different reality, where education is characterised by intellectual rigour first. However, all three students are aligned in seeing difficulty and challenge as core educational values, which neither individualism, nor attempts at a kind of assessment populism, should trump.

For junior and teaching-focused staff, a plurality of responsibilities was often acknowledged as part and parcel of modern university life. Teaching fellow Betka felt the pull of both inspirational and employment-driven concerns, both of which were important for the aspirational liberal arts students at her post-war institution, and connected this to her own path to academia:

> 'I mean, as a student, I was a really traditional student. I loved theories. Still do, you know? And I loved to do non-practical things and no exercises and no involvement, no discussions. I hated that, you know? So, now I'm teaching on things that – but having ... started working and having zero knowledge of working skills, I wish that somebody told me at the time, you know, that, actually, it would be really handy to know how to do teamwork or whatever.'

We will come back to Betka's sense of responsibility for preparing her students for work shortly. For now, we can note that a plurality of values that are merely *celebrated* on liberal arts websites ('There are countless reasons why you might like to study [this degree]; to study across the disciplines, learn a new language or give yourself a step up on the competitive graduate job market. These are just a few – read on for more' [website, old]) are experienced in more complex and ambivalent ways by both students and junior academics.

What's in a name? Explaining the liberal arts

'So, normally, I would say, "I do liberal arts. Do you know what that is?"' (Phoebe, fourth-year student, post-war)

For students studying liberal arts degrees, one serious challenge is the lack of recognition the name receives, whether from schoolteachers, parents, other students or potential employers. Misunderstandings abound; for instance, that it's fine art ("Oh, can you draw?" [Jessica, third-year student, old]) or expressive arts ("They think I do sort of dancing" [Phoebe, fourth-year student, post-war]), or that it is chosen as a cop-out ("a bit of a doss" [Devendra, fourth-year student, old]) and, where sciences are included, "'Sciences' kind of often falls off" (Ellie, second-year student, old). It's important to note that students' concerns about the name of the degree, especially in the eyes of employers (its market value), are not by any means the same as a lack of belief in the value of the degree and the education itself – but both are important for students.

As we saw earlier, Devendra was sceptical about the job prospects for his fellow students who had studied only the humanities and had failed to take up the opportunity to develop more technical skills. He discussed his choice to major in chemistry as follows: "I guess people think that the analytical skills, the numerical literacy, the relevance of it perhaps in aspects: particularly my project is very commercially relevant. … I just felt it had more academic weight to it. People would have thought I'd probably had to work a lot harder." Here, Devendra seems to refer to what makes the *substance* of a chemistry degree valid; yet, he really couches this in terms of what people think having a degree in chemistry signals. Indeed, elsewhere, he cast doubt on the personal value of the subject for him, noting that it "felt like the drag on my degree, and everything else I've done, which have been the arts and humanities, have been the stuff I've enjoyed". The dividing line between the market notion of employability and the industrial one, which concentrates on the qualities actually needed to be a good worker, then, was sometimes blurred in students' accounts.

Other students tended to be strategic when managing the riskiness of the degree on the job market. Second-year student Konstantina, for instance, had spent lots of time applying for different summer internships. She was taking a very wide range of modules as part of her liberal arts degree at an old institution and focused on different courses depending on the post she was applying for:

'Every time I apply for a photography job, I will write, "[liberal arts]: modules include photography", which I've done; "anthropology". You know, the arty things I've done. When I apply for environmental conservation jobs, which is also something I'm very interested in, I will put, "[liberal arts]: modules include geography, environmental systems and societies, physics of the Earth". Which I've all done, but you can manipulate it.'

The naming of the major or pathway in the degree title can also prove an important compromise between the liberal arts and traditional disciplines. We have seen that student Lijuan had strongly inspirational values and wished to disentangle what she thought of as the true purpose of education from mere workplace preparation. Yet, she nonetheless used the availability of a more clearly recognisable disciplinary major as a strategy to convince her parents to allow her to take the course: "I also told them, 'I can graduate my degree with stuff saying "major in physics", and that's helpful.' I actually don't know whether that's helpful or not, but I just told them that."

This suggests that while students are aware of a liberal arts degree's potentially tricky reception on the job market, market values are certainly not all that is going on. Indeed, the fact that students choose the degree *despite* concerns about market worth demonstrates the plural values they bring to bear. At modern institutions, in particular, the tension between being attractive to employers and staying true to a more inspirational sense of what the liberal arts are all about was keenly felt. The promotional websites of such institutions do not gloss over these problems, but seek to make them explicit. Likewise, third-year student Jen talked about this tension at her modern institution, which was addressed by both staff and students:

'And there is a – I think there is a slight resistance in some way of not wanting to sell ourselves, but then also knowing that we exist in the real world and we're going to need jobs. So, I do find there is definitely a tension there, of wanting to keep some – I don't know – some sort of the liberal arts education alive, but also being able to utilise that in a way that can then allow you to get a job.'

The unknown future of work

> Schools can prepare [young people] for jobs that have not yet been created, for technologies that have not yet been invented, to solve problems that have not yet been anticipated. (Organisation for Economic Co-operation and Development, 2019: 127)

The sense that the future is open and must be shaped by our decision making in the present – rather than that it will be determined by blind fate – is a key feature of modernity (Luhmann, 1976, 1998). In this context, education takes a central role in preparing people to be ready for this open future. Increasingly, this preparation for the future is understood in terms of the workplace: the industrial order's 'worker of tomorrow' (Boltanski and Thévenot, 2006: 205); yet, it is also intimately bound up with notions of what it means to be a good subject in general. In this section, we will look at how liberal arts degrees are imagined in relation to this future on promotional websites and, in more complex ways, by students from less privileged backgrounds and academics at modern institutions. For while the conceptualisation of the future of work found on websites tends to stress the supply side of the equation ('What is it that makes some students employable?'), some students without financial safety nets draw our attention to the demand side ('Where are the jobs?').

The imaginary future to which liberal arts degrees at more elite institutions point is what has been termed 'VUCA' (that is, a volatile, uncertain, complex and ambiguous one). Given this sense of perpetual change and unknowability, what is required of education's subjects is an ability to deal with unknowability and change itself, rather than any specific knowledge: '[this degree] will provide the adaptability and flexibility you need in our rapidly changing world' (website, old). Irrespective of the difficulties of establishing whether life is 'more' volatile than it used to be (presumably in the post-war period), or even quite what this means, this narrative is central to understanding not only how the liberal arts are sold, but also to how many students think about their futures.[1]

The liberal arts are said to be well suited to the unknown and volatile future because of the flexibility required to move between disciplines and the concomitant focus on 'learning to learn'. Rather than specific content, or even specific skills like coding (which may quickly become outdated),

---

[1] One episode of BBC Radio 4's (2017) statistics programme 'More or less' sought to unpack the oft-made claim that '65% of jobs that will exist in a generation's time haven't been invented yet'. It eventually came to the conclusion that, even if we take the generous view that the statement can be made to mean something, it isn't true.

the development of competences like these is thought to prepare students for a world in which the only known is unknowability. As Saad, who had just graduated from his liberal arts degree at an old institution, explained:

> 'Because if I picture myself, or pigeon-hole myself, as an accountant or a doctor right now, I think it's a stable career and it always has been, but it's hard to say in 20 years' time if it will be the same. Whereas if you've got the skills to adapt to different kinds of careers, I'd be in a better position.'

As Elena Esposito (2015: 102) writes: 'One does not know which future will come, but one can count on having a strategy for any of them.'

Since the future is unknown, the liberal arts are preparing students for any number of interesting jobs. Moreover, since the liberal arts student has wisely rejected specialist training, the future is conceived of on institutions' promotional websites as an open horizon upon which there is an infinite array of options: 'By studying Liberal Arts at [this university], you'll learn key skills that can be applied to any position in industry or future study' (website, post-war); and '[This degree] really can take you just about anywhere you'd like to go to do anything you'd like to do!' (website, old).

Statements like these always put me in mind of some university careers events I've attended that begin with the rictus-grinned line that 'Even sociology graduates!' can apply to these jobs. Yes, they can apply. But is this quite the question students are asking?

Student Konstantina had come to study in England from Greece and had known economic downturn and recession since she was very young. She spoke with great insight about the reality of the job market, even for graduates of apparently 'safe' degrees like law. It was a requirement on her liberal arts course that she should complete a summer internship between her second and third years, yet she had submitted hundreds of applications without success. Keeping her 'failure' a secret until she eventually discovered that her friends were all in the same boat, she expressed her suspicion that the cruel optimism (Berlant, 2011) of the 'You could do anything!' narrative fed students' secrecy and self-blame. She spoke of a desire that universities be more honest about what any degree will be able to assure in terms of jobs:

> 'But also, I think, honestly, we don't have as many options: it's so competitive. But no one told me that. I had no idea because I left Greece to come to [this university], which is one of the best universities, so I felt that I would find a job immediately. So, now, I've seen so many people from my degree have struggled – but not only my degree, honestly, from any degree – have struggled so much to find jobs that we realise more and more that we don't have as many options. It's not

really a matter of what you want to do. It's a matter of what you can find, and do it.'

If we understand all graduates, even all graduates from prestigious universities, as a self-contained elite to whom access to privileged jobs is relatively guaranteed (as some universities encourage applicants to think), then we are likely to be baffled by their apparent failure to secure 'graduate work'. If, conversely, we acknowledge that the graduate labour market is not a phenomenon discrete from the broader labour market (Tholen, 2014) and that the likelihood of securing a certain type of job is first dependent on how many jobs of that sort there are and how many people are likely to apply for them, then we will be able to be more honest with students about what we can and cannot know about the future. In the actually existing labour market, most graduates will fall into what Patrick Ainley (2016a: 4) calls the 'workingmiddle' class – neither high fliers nor poorly paid – not because they lack the abilities to do more executive or creative roles (a kind of 'supply-side fundamentalism' [Peck and Theodore, 2000: 729]), but simply because this middling range is where the jobs are. The reality for most workers is at least some degree of routine, even drudgery at times; knowledge work is not above the Taylorist forces that tend to limit avenues for creativity and autonomy for the majority (Brown et al, 2015), however hard we are bombarded with images of a minority of knowledge workers blue-sky thinking around smart whiteboards or taking power naps in hammocks. If students hear next to nothing about this type of work, it will continue to be understood as a booby prize, resorted to once the effort to secure (what are perceived as) graduate jobs has failed.

The idea that the non-specialisation of the liberal arts presents a particularly appealing prospect for university applicants was also questioned by some academics. Pro-vice chancellor Alan explained that while he was very aware of the unknown future narrative, he had not found it effective at his modern university:

'"People go off and go into all sorts of jobs. If you don't know what you want to do then do this." So, obviously, you try and sell that story, but I'm not convinced that that connects directly with the discourse that's used by parents or careers advisers, or teaching mentors or whatever, you know.'

Alan works at a teaching-focused institution and seems more connected to the desires and motivations of comprehensive and first-generation students than the celebratory blurbs on the websites of more elite institutions quoted earlier. Indeed, contra the idea that the liberal arts would prepare students for the jobs of the future, some parents with little personal experience of higher education had tried to convince students that the market value of a degree should trump any concern with the actual content of the course or skills imparted. Third-year student Lijuan's parents in China were not familiar with English higher education but knew that the link between a recognisable degree and employment was important: "[My parents] don't really know what I learned in economics [at A level], and they don't really know what's gonna be taught in economics [at university]; they just know economics is gonna get me a job."

Some more privileged students understood the unknown future of work as a story they told in certain contexts, rather than a personal value. Will, finishing his degree at a post-war institution, related his reluctance to rely on this story to a wish not to be cynical about higher education:

'You can also link it to employability as well, so if someone is quite miserably cynical about how the nature of learning works, then you can just sort of suggest that most people in their life do more than ten different jobs and [have] a wide array of interests, and so it's quite useful that you have good writing skills as well as good analytics. But I try to use that one as the last resort.'

The ways that universities sell ideas about the future of work are, then, bought into and also critiqued by both students and staff, depending on their security in relation to the job market. The relentlessly cheery focus on individual aspiration on websites, or the supply side of the equation ('With such a relevant portfolio, you will walk into the United Nations feeling very confident about your job interview' [website, old]) ignores the demand side; that is, that 'it is possible to be employable but not be in employment' (Brown et al, 2003: 122).

Furthermore, while some students were very insightful or humorous about the reality of the job market, others had clearly been influenced by the world-as-oyster narrative. For instance, the Civil Service Fast Stream is regularly invoked as an employment possibility at universities, both for liberal arts students and, more generally, in the humanities and social sciences. This message had been absorbed by many students, and the Fast Stream was mentioned in a vague way by students without concrete plans after graduation. Yet, the scheme is extremely competitive, accepting just 3.8 per cent of applicants in 2016. (Although it's not all bad news: this rises to 10.6 per cent if an Oxbridge graduate and 28.6 per cent if privately educated [Institute for Government, 2018]). The future is indeed unknown, but this does not mean that a degree in liberal arts will open every potential door irrespective of labour market conditions or structural inequalities.

Strategies to manage the unknown: anxiety, forbearance and control

> 'There's no point in planning what you're going to do in ten years because you might be dead.' (Konstantina, second-year student, old)

The sense of the future as unknown can have radically different effects on individuals. For some, spontaneity, autonomy and flexibility find a seamless continuity with their subjectivity: they 'have happily sacrificed desires for security and routines idealized in the second spirit of capitalism for the excitement of constant activity idealized in the new spirit of capitalism' (Jensen, 2018: 279). However, for many others, this match between subjectivity and environment is incomplete and fraught with tensions. In this section, I discuss three broad strategies for thinking about the unknown future among students: anxiety, forbearance and control. Pertinent here are different relationships to risk (Brynin, 2012) and to its concomitant angst, conditioned by social class among other differences (Schmitz et al, 2018).

Clearly, all young people (indeed, all people) experience anxiety about the future's unknowability. The sheer range of options, far from creating a sense of open-eyed wonder, as in the narratives on elite universities' websites, can mean that making decisions about the future is deeply fraught. Bianca, now in the third year of her liberal arts degree at a post-war university, rather breathlessly recounted the difficulties of choosing what to study at university, eventually making the decision to study liberal arts in order to delay the decision-making process altogether:

> 'I'm from South Africa, and I finished high school and I had applied for university in South Africa. But I had applied for a degree in architecture and a degree in astrophysics, [and] just a general BA, and I had an offer of one of [each of] those three at [a university] over there because those were kind of, you know, my broad interests. And I liked physics, but I also really liked architecture. ... I just really – I didn't know, and I – and in the end, I decided not to do any of that because the decision just felt too big to go between either one of those things and to kind of exclude that other one completely.'

The fact that the liberal arts left many doors open was appealing to Bianca because it offered a way of managing anxiety by delaying the decision. For first-generation students in particular, however, the narrative of generic preparation for a range of jobs did not offer a reassuring delay, but rather *increased* anxiety, as alluded to by pro-vice chancellor Alan earlier. Such students specifically contrasted this unpredictable career trajectory with the 'standard adulthood' narrative of their parents or grandparents, in which a job for life was central to the transition out of youth (Blatterer, 2007). Contrasted to this particular set of post-war experiences – generally extended in the imagination so that it felt as if in *all* previous generations, *all* workers could expect a job for life – the decision to take a degree predicated on the notion of an unknown future was difficult. As Lithuanian student Veronika, whose family had no experience with higher education and who had recently enrolled on a liberal arts course at an old institution, explained:

> 'It took me a year to apply actually because I was insecure and I wasn't too convinced by the fact that I would not really specialise in something. So [pause], I come from a family in which no one really pursued academia, so nobody really understands how universities work. But I was encouraged into the thought that I would need to pursue one career and that would be my career from university to pension.'

Websites don't always ignore this anxiety; rather, they may acknowledge it while encouraging risk-*taking* as the best way to mitigate against the risky future:

> I know that this can be a stressful time, especially as you weigh various course offers and try to imagine the routes your life can take. We want to encourage you to take risks, to dream big, and to make your decision out of hope and determination, not stress or anxiety. (Website, post-war)

Here, our relationship to risk-taking is a complex one: it is the taking of the risk that brings about, not the mourned-for certainty ("It's becoming less and less clear to me what I would really like to do after uni" [Lotte, first-year student, old]), but rather acceptance of the uncertainty itself. For instance, Bianca (third-year student, post-war), who, as we saw, chose liberal arts because she couldn't decide between architecture and astrophysics, was still struggling with anxiety and ambivalence about her degree by her third year when I talked to her. Yet, she now valued the experience for teaching her to be more flexible and less disturbed by uncertainty: "You're able to deal with everything that comes your way and kind of manage within that." The key is to regard oneself as incomplete and in a constant process of becoming (Andersen, 2007), a kind of spontaneous, inspirational mode where one's future self can be trusted.

Those with a more secure safety net than first-generation student Veronika often suggested a kind of tacit knowhow about the job market and were already developing complex portfolio careers without a clear end point in mind. Such students often considered it better to be on the bottom rung of a ladder that presented the prospect of an interesting future – much like the highly strategic middle-class graduates in Ciaran Burke's (2016) study – rather than getting 'stuck' in a job for life. Many of the students from more privileged backgrounds described a mixture of general activity in a range of fields, along with their social capital, as what would propel them into the future, without necessarily knowing what that future would entail. Sophie, for instance, had experienced a mix of public and private schooling, going on to choose a private institution for her degree. Only in her second year, she was proactively engaged in creating a future that remained unknowable:

> 'I mean, I haven't heard any of my friends say, "This is what I want to get into", "These are the steps I need to take." We're all sort of working jobs or doing things that perhaps don't relate to our degree, just try and make contacts, things like that. So, it is a sense that we're a bit lost and all over the place, but I don't think that's negative, at least for me. It just means I have good time to figure things out and I can sort of do what I enjoy for the moment.' (Sophie, second-year student, private)

While the future's unknowability might be internalised in a rather flippant way for some, more privileged students (as Will put it: "That's the 'too long; don't read'. I don't have a bloody clue, but I'm quite comfortable"), for those without the comfort of a safety net, it can develop into an almost melancholic sanguinity. Second-year student Konstantina's family in Greece had suffered from the recession, and as we have seen, she had a complex relationship with the liberal arts as preparation for the future:

> 'That's why I don't think there is a point in planning so much. Perhaps sometimes it's just – focus on the present and things will bring – one thing will bring the next, I think. I don't know ... I think my generation, we've just adapted to the circumstances, and whatever we can find we're happy, and we've tried our best.' (Konstantina, second-year student, old)

This is an intensification of the cheery fatalism expressed by some of Blatterer's (2007) young participants 15 years ago, deepened by the experience of recession. In order for modern meritocracy to function, it requires notions of openness, growth, hard work and change: to believe that my position in the future has already been determined by some preordained 'talent', or indeed by fate, would be to opt out of the competitive impulse that keeps the meritocratic struggle in motion (Allen, 2014). Yet, this narrative of agency and responsibility is complexly entangled with a large chunk of humility about one's ability to control the future. I am obliged to work actively to forge a future, but I must not imagine that I can predict how anything will turn out in the end. This recognition of the future's contingency is, paradoxically, one of the only *necessities* of modern life (Roitman, 2013).

It is possible, however, to overstate the extent to which young people have internalised the narrative of mindful living in the moment and acceptance of the unknown future. When we conceive of generations in simplistic ways (for instance, short-handing to 'Generation Z'), we are likely to miss the complexity of their experiences (Williams, 2020). For some students, industrial values of stability, certainty and predictability remained central. State-school student Saad, for instance, discussed the way he had planned for his future throughout the degree he was just finishing at an old institution and talked about his reluctance to buy into the 'serendipitous' philosophy of some of his more privileged peers: "And if I sort of just coast and see where the wind takes me, I'll end up just working in professional services. There's nothing wrong with that, but it's not what I wanted. So, I always felt I had to really start planning early and take the right steps."

This attempt to plan for a stable future was especially pronounced for those state-educated students, like Natasha, who were also the first in their family to go to university. Natasha connected her desire for a single, steady career to her concern with social justice – the impact her work would have on others was foregrounded over thoughts about what might be fulfilling for herself:

> 'To pick a sort of path that I'll stick on. So, because, like I said, I want to sort of have an impact and I feel like you need to sort of work at something for a long time for it to actually make a concrete difference. I'm not expecting to go straight into a job and change the world overnight.'

Lecturers, especially junior ones who worked closely with large numbers of students, often felt that instilling a philosophical acceptance of uncertainty was a key part of their job. They taught that, as post-war teaching fellow Betka put it, "You can only try. Just keep doing the best you can, for that moment." She described her own younger self's lack of preparedness for the world of work but, more generally, wanted to encourage her students to live in the present and feel less concern for the future and for "all those factors that are external". In a sense, she sought here to pull her students reassuringly forward into a future that she already inhabited, something that websites also do in their use of student and graduate testimonials: 'At times my subject and module choices seemed quite random, but looking back, my choices have made more sense than I ever realised' (student testimonial, website, old). It is an invitation to trust the future, which makes sense from the perspective of those who already inhabit it but may not always be felt as reassurance by those still in the anxious throes of uncertainty. As Mathilde, a second-year student at an old institution, reflected: "It might be useful to get more advice, to get something a bit more coherent, because we do want a job after this."

While institutions' promotional websites, then, hail the future's unknowability as a call 'to take risks, to dream big' (website, post-war) and confront uncertainty head-on, students' relationships to the future world of work are much more ambivalent. Even for those, often from more privileged backgrounds, for whom uncertainty can be inhabited mindfully – and even with a kind of pleasure – this has the potential to tip over into fear, melancholy and eventually nihilism. There is a problem when particular ways of relating to the world, such as a kind of corporate-friendly mindfulness, are presented not as options, but as demands – and when they become the only way to be received as a well-functioning subject (Claus et al, 2018).

Conclusion

To think about students' relationships to their future employment as characterised by cynical calculation, so that they choose a degree merely on a market consideration of what that degree may later be traded for, is to miss the plurality of their thoughts. Even if students *wanted* to be this cynical, it's actually very difficult to make a calculation about the 'return' on the investment of a degree, or to predict what job or jobs it may lead to (Brynin, 2012).

Nor should we understand students as good neoliberal subjects who buy into the mantras of adaptability, mindfulness and the portfolio career that they are often sold, both on institutions' promotional websites and elsewhere. It is crucial to bear in mind the incomplete nature of most individuals' reconciliation to modern capitalism. Students are humorous, insightful and deeply ambivalent about their futures and the work they will contain, *especially* those students who do not fit the model of a privately educated home student with a financial safety net. However, to acknowledge all this is not to say that they don't (or *shouldn't*) care about work.

And among all this employability talk, whither the employer? There is a kind of 'corporate impatience' (Brown et al, 2011: 87) in the assumption that the burden of 'employability' should fall, first, on the shoulders of students themselves and, second, upon the university. It seems to have been accepted by politicians and university managers that a key function of higher education is a free employee-preparation scheme for the corporate world (invariably criticised by its beneficiaries as not up to muster). The generally accepted idea is that the graduate should already be ready to go into employment (Brown and Hesketh, 2004), and, increasingly, the higher education *applicant* is expected to be ready to go too (Burke and McManus, 2011). To think of students as mere consumers of higher education, preparing themselves for the demands of tomorrow's workplace, however, is to miss many aspects of their multifaceted identities, as we will explore in Chapter 5.

5

Identity and the 'ideal' student: citizens, cosmopolitans, consumers?

In this chapter, we will examine three different ways that liberal arts students' identities are constructed on institutions' promotional websites, by academics of different stripes and by students themselves. The first is as good citizens: the idea that the liberal arts approach to education creates politically engaged and critical (but respectful) individuals with a concern for social justice. The second, connected student identity is the cosmopolitan: the well-travelled, and therefore open-minded, citizen of the world. Finally, we turn to the idea of the consumer student. This refrain, which can often be heard in relation to England's fee regime, suggests that modern students consider themselves to have *bought* a degree and that they appeal to their consumer rights whenever they are dissatisfied with their product.

You might notice that these are quite different sorts of student identity, for while citizenship and cosmopolitanism are generally thought of as positive attributes, a consumerist mentality is not. The purpose of bringing them together in this way is to show how a hierarchy of ambivalence operates differently in different contexts.

I have argued throughout the book that there is an inverse relationship between power and insight, so that, for instance, modern institutions' promotional websites tend to seek to disentangle complex value systems in ways that the websites of old and post-war universities do not. Similarly, students in interviews offer insights about what is the most appropriate educational value to bring to bear in particular contexts, which academics may instead glide over. Even further than this, those students who are at some remove from the supposedly traditional higher education student (by virtue of class, ethnicity or nationality, for instance) work harder to pull apart different values in order to make claims about what is important in a particular context and what is not, in comparison to more privileged students; the same can be said for junior academics as opposed to those who are more senior. The three aspects of liberal arts students' identities discussed in turn in this chapter (citizenship, cosmopolitanism and consumerism) build from one another in such a way that we are able to see these processes of disentanglement move from the gentler to the more significant.

The chapter begins by examining claims made on institutions' promotional websites, as well as in some interviews, about the links between the liberal arts approach and a concern for social justice. As we have found in previous chapters, there is an easy and often unspoken entanglement of ideas about interdisciplinarity, open-mindedness, left-wingery and good citizenship here. As we have also seen in previous chapters, this was portrayed more carefully, and in more questioning ways, on the promotional websites of modern, as opposed to old or post-war, institutions. The link between citizenship and the liberal arts was also *very* gently critiqued by some students and academics in interviews through an acknowledgement that this link may appear moralistic or 'preachy' to those on the outside of it.

One specific way that the inherent goodness of the liberal arts student is presented is via the image of the *cosmopolitan* citizen, who stands opposed, both on liberal arts websites and in the accounts of some senior academics, to the narrow-minded and the disciplinary. More so than the previous aspect of good citizenship, in the specific case of cosmopolitanism, some students (especially state-educated or first-generation students) seek to disentangle ideas about moral goodness from ones about geographical mobility. While I am critical here of the narrative that equates geographical mobility with open-mindedness (and can slip quite comfortably from here to class-based assessments), I also try to unpack the opposite argument, heard from some, that would set an international elite against a more economically modest cohort of home students. The assumption that mobility and openness are connected in obvious ways is what animates both of these apparently opposed ideas about student cosmopolitanism.

The second half of the chapter moves away from such straightforwardly positive depictions of the ideal liberal arts student (and the unpickings of students themselves) and towards an aspect of student identity that has proven particularly perturbing for politicians, institutions, academics and students alike: consumerism. However, while institutional websites tend to promote the liberal arts as in keeping with consumerist ideas like student satisfaction and individual choice (albeit not described as consumerism), and while some senior academics decried the consumerism of today's students, both students themselves and those academics with more close contact with them engaged with apparently consumerist ideas in ways that were far more thoughtful, ambivalent and nuanced. Here, my argument is that far from emanating *from* students, a consumerist mindset is actively fostered by institutions' promotional attempts.

These are quite different ways of thinking about the modern student's identity, then. However, in all three cases, I argue, institutions promote simplistic and problematic descriptions of students that do our actually existing students a great disservice.

Good citizens: liberal arts as social justice

As I have been learning about systems and making a sustainable impact on my course for two years now, I found my experience with [this university] in Africa not only a challenging and rewarding experience on a personal level, but also an edifying field trip academically and career-wise. (Student testimonial, website, post-war)

In modern Europe the three essential requirements of social integration, the enhancement of employability and personal fulfilment, are not incompatible. They should not be brought into conflict, but should on the contrary be closely linked. (European Commission, 1995: 4)

There is a significant literature in the US linking a liberal arts education to notions of citizenship. To use one of the most well-known examples, Martha Nussbaum (2010) has argued that some of the key tenets of the liberal arts approach and, in particular, the Socratic teaching method, provide an important training for full participation in civic life. Many promotional websites for such degrees in England, in turn, appeal to notions of the liberal arts as an education for citizenship: 'A Liberal Arts education is based on the idea of acquiring knowledge and understanding worthy of a free, active and engaged global citizen' (website, post-war).

We might think of this idea of citizenship education as fundamentally concerned with the *common* good and thus implying a clear division between the public and private spheres; however, in practice, civic ideas are not left to stand alone, but tend instead to be tied in to both personal employment concerns and a more general project of individual self-development. On the websites of post-war and old institutions, as in the epigraph to this section, becoming a good citizen, especially through social justice activities, is thought of as an individual life project: 'it's up to you to choose what matters, which issues inspire you, which causes are worth pursuing and which areas of knowledge you need to acquire in order to effect change' (website, post-war). This entangles civic values of public service with the inspirational values of a personally meaningful life, as if neither could exist without the other.

In examples like the preceding quotation, concerns with social justice are conceived of as *projects*: discrete, often time-limited and generally goal-oriented activities, resulting in positive change for both the world out there and the individual in here. In this way, social justice projects are not dissimilar to other sorts of projects of the self and can be mentioned in the same breath as work, education, creative expression and even hobbies as all the things a person is doing to make up a full life. Third-year student Asif, for instance, described the varied interests of a friend on the liberal arts degree at his old university. This student's project for social justice was part of a longer list of meaningful activities:

'There's this guy X who is like learning Mandarin Chinese; is a great music producer. Also, he's on this research scholarship for doing interviews with Philippine women who had to leave to other countries in order to supply – be the breadwinner for their family as well. He's also a really amazing ocean engineer as well, and that's probably what he's going to go into. I'm like, "Man, what? Like, what are you doing?"'

While ideas about civic values are knotted into highly individualist ones about personal life projects, then, the stick is also bent the other way; that is, fostering citizenship in the individual is thought to lead to a socially just society. Beyond educating a small number of individuals for social leadership roles, the liberal arts approach is regarded as a *democratic* good because it contributes more broadly to an educated citizenry:

> At heart, it's about a citizenry that is educated enough not just to offer up capable candidates for public office, but also is able to act as a check on government figures. It's about educating citizens for a highly participatory civic system, and that's the philosophy that has driven the development of Liberal Arts at [this university]. (Website, post-war)

Here, we get a sense that, as in the motto often attributed to University of Chicago President Robert Maynard Hutchins, 'The best education for the best [is] the best education for all' (quoted in, among others, Adler, 1988: 310); that is, that education for citizenship should be available to all in the service of democracy.

Yet, on post-war and old institutions' websites, the notion of the liberal arts as preparation for *leadership* remains a strong selling point, with the idea being that the generic skills of communication, big-picture thinking and the rest make one particularly suited to elite roles: 'A liberal arts approach gives you the skills, knowledge and creativity necessary to succeed as the *next generation of global thinkers, leaders and innovators*' (website, old, emphasis in original). The notion that the liberal arts would provide a good education for all citizens is bound in a knot, then, with the idea of social hierarchy required to give 'leadership' its meaning (unless we are all to become leaders, with none left to be led). In Hutchins's apparently democratic motto, we retain a notion of the best students, even while allowing their educational deserts to trickle down to the masses.

The websites of more elite institutions often link the liberal arts approach's concern with social justice to interdisciplinarity. It is, as we saw in Chapter 2, part of a hyper-interdisciplinary view that gives interdisciplinarity a distinctly moral (rather than merely epistemological or practical) advantage over the fusty old disciplines (Moore, 2011). This entanglement implicitly connects the fact that interdisciplinarity entails looking at an issue from multiple perspectives both to a solution-oriented practicality and on, again, to social justice: 'Often, the most robust solutions are found through collaboration and understanding the problem from different perspectives. As such, [liberal arts] is an ideal place to start for any student hoping to make the world a better place' (website, old).

Students' relationships to such entanglements of value tended to be quite different from those on promotional websites. For Natasha, choosing a degree that aligned with her own social justice imperatives, including what she hoped to do for work, was important. However, she was very considered in her response to my question about whether certain types of people might be attracted to the liberal arts. Noting that she felt her answer to the question was "obviously complete conjecture", one possible characteristic mentioned was "open-mindedness". When asked a follow-up question on this, Natasha responded:

> 'People that apply for that sort of degree are already thinking about the world in interdisciplinary ways, and if you mean open-minded and sort of – like I said, most of the people [in] my year are quite sort of lefty. I don't know if that's for – I don't think that's necessarily because of – it might be because of our core modules focusing on social justice.'

Where citizenship and social justice *were* important to students' conceptions of their degree, this often happened in highly reflective and self-deprecating ways. As Natasha went on to say: "It sounds quite cheesy to be like, 'I want to do something that makes a difference.' It's a very uni student thing." In his interview, dean Larry spent some time distinguishing between the ideal student for the liberal arts degree at his old institution (curious, independent and public-spirited) from the student who simply cannot decide what to study. However, like Natasha, he went on to deprecate himself: "It's probably too preachy to talk about commitment and, you know, noble ideals of public service and all the rest of it. Sounds quite Victorian."

Both Larry and Natasha pointed out that their immediately preceding ideas about the liberal arts and citizenship may *sound* like something that no one would want to be: neither "quite cheesy" nor "quite Victorian" are descriptors that most people would welcome. They put their cynical hats on for a moment; however, this does not mean that they have stopped being idealist about the relationship between education and social change. This is because idealism and cynicism, as I argued in the Introduction, are not two extremes on one scale (Allen, 2017), but rather parts of different registers upon which we can draw. The donning of cynical hats was perhaps prompted by a perception of me as a cynical sociologist unlikely to hold much truck with such idealism (Cassell, 2005). However, to say that this self-deprecation has something to do with the interview itself is not to say that it is an artefact of it (Hughes et al, 2020); rather, Larry and Natasha demonstrate a reflective recognition that somebody might receive their idealism more cynically and thus demonstrate their awareness of multiple value systems. To say 'it sounds like' is a way of acknowledging this interpretation's legitimacy while maintaining that it is not the whole story.

In different ways, a number of students pointed to the fact that the relationship between the liberal arts and social justice is not as straightforward as might be inferred from the public pronouncements of universities. While the idea of liberal arts education as citizenship education was something they had heard lecturers stress, it was clearly not at the forefront of some students' minds at all. Victoria was in the same year at the same old institution as Natasha; yet, unlike her fellow student, she made a clear distinction between the institutional entanglement of good citizenship with interdisciplinarity and many students' concerns:

'It's definitely what the liberal arts department promote. It's like, they've got like a big poster … and it's all about, like, "Are we gonna fix the world?" Which I think is probably one of the very good reasons for the degree; like, appeal of it. But it's not something I've heard other people say.'

Some made a more political point about the problems of associating the liberal arts with social justice too easily. Agathe was a French student with Algerian heritage, entering her final year at a post-war institution. She wished to question the easy entanglement of her degree with social justice concerns, which meant, she thought, that it could blithely appeal to relatively privileged white students who were "very loud about their anti-colonialism, anti-racism". (On how the historical association between some universities and leftist student politics, often exploited in institutions' promotional attempts, can appeal to privileged students in particular, see Francesca Bartram's [2020] thoughtful work.)

While some students seek to unpick the values of social justice from their blithe entanglement with the liberal arts, there is also an important difference between more and less elite institutions' websites. On modern universities' sites, there is often a more measured approach to social justice (or perhaps what Larry called "public service" earlier), focusing on duty over individual flourishing: 'We take seriously the idea that the best graduates, and those most valued by employers, are those who have developed for themselves a set of principles that will guide their conduct and most especially the decisions that will affect the lives of others' (website, modern).

While the entanglement of civic and more inspirational, individualist values goes unremarked on old and post-war institutions' websites, then, the websites of modern universities, as well as students themselves, tell more complicated stories about the liberal arts and social justice. The blithe acceptance of the former that interdisciplinarity, by virtue of its polymathy, leads to an open-minded and progressive mentality for *all*, irrespective of whether individual students identify with this, can result in peculiar juxtapositions of communality and individualism, as when claims are made for 'a community of ambitious, focused and forward-looking students, who are keen to chart their own path through education and who, like you, share the qualities of open-mindedness, alertness and maturity' (website, post-war). As we will see in more detail in the next section, this notion of progressiveness-in-common can have problematic consequences, especially when it implies (or explicitly invokes) a regressive 'outside' of such community.

Cosmopolitans and parochials: the limits of open-mindedness

A specific type of citizenship that is often connected to a liberal arts education in the English and broader European context is cosmopolitanism (see, for example, Harward, 2018). The term 'cosmopolitanism' can be used to refer to a wide range of things, from the presence of a nationally diverse cohort, to a curricular focus (for example, through foreign language options or, in some cases, requirements), study abroad or some rather vaguer sense that the liberal arts are cosmopolitan because they aren't a very English idea.

As with the broader ideas about social justice in the previous section, the prizing of cosmopolitanism is not only related to being prepared for work, but also tied in with the development of a well-rounded subjecthood. For some senior academics, the choice of the liberal arts might be connected to a more general open-mindedness, as contrasted with the narrow-mindedness of what one dean called "little Englandism". The importance of geographical mobility was, however, challenged by some students: by first-generation students with a sense of some particular place as home; and by others for whom the international nature of the degrees covered over, or even fostered, a significant homogeneity of *class*. These entanglements are particularly complex, however, as in the very act of bringing attention to class, we can easily gloss over inequalities that disadvantage international students, irrespective of socio-economic background.

A concern with cosmopolitanism runs all the way through how the liberal arts are promoted on institutions' websites: it is a characteristic that those who *choose* such degrees are said to have; the degree is presented as a cosmopolitan *experience*; and, finally, liberal arts graduates are said to have *become* cosmopolitan citizens. The scale of this cosmopolitanism is captured well in the following:

> Being part of our highly international student body gives you the chance to make new friends from diverse backgrounds, learn about different cultures and practise your linguistic skills. This is your opportunity to build a valuable international network that will set

you apart from other graduates before even entering the professional world. (Website, private)

In promotional attempts like this, cosmopolitanism is explicitly connected to the job market. This is seen even more clearly where degrees contain a foreign language requirement, with language acquisition presented here as a highly marketable graduate attribute:

[The liberal arts department] regards achievement in a foreign language as central to the future generation of careers. Whether it is working with the growing economies of China, India, the Middle East or South America, working in Europe or interrelating to British nationals in an increasingly diverse society, skill in a foreign language is a key part of a university degree. (Website, old)

This is what Don Weenink (2008) calls cosmopolitan*ation*, rather than cosmopolitanism: a strategic acknowledgement that such qualities are needed to get ahead, as opposed to a philosophical, political or ethical commitment to a cosmopolitan way of life.

However, in many cases, cosmopolitanism is not merely invoked by websites in this instrumental or even cynical way. Rather, it is often folded somewhat casually into broader concerns with the fostering of a certain character, notions of intellectual ability or a long list of graduate attributes. Since the link with cosmopolitanism in such lists is often assumed, rather than spelt out, it is not always clear what 'international', 'global' or 'cosmopolitan' is precisely doing in the sentence: 'A liberal arts education is based on the idea of acquiring knowledge and understanding worthy of a free, active and engaged global citizen' (website, post-war); 'You must be of the highest intellectual calibre, and we are looking for a commitment to embrace the challenge of a truly cosmopolitan education' (website, old); or 'You will have two academic specialisms, strong leadership and communication skills and the ability to work flexibly, creatively and internationally in a range of fields' (website, old).

It is too simplistic, then, to say that cosmopolitanism is invoked merely as a type of capital for the job market; in the preceding examples, it is being folded much more intimately into some ill-defined sense of personhood. We are not merely in the realms of job market values or of preparation-for-work values, but, as we have seen throughout, concerned with a knot of different sorts of value tangled together.

In interviews too, and much like notions of citizenship and social justice in the previous section, those involved in liberal arts degrees mentioned the nationally diverse student body, or their interest in travel, quite casually, within lists of the personal attributes of liberal arts students and, again, in particular conjunction with open-mindedness. First-year student Lotte, for instance, had chosen to come to a diverse city in England from her home in the Netherlands partially to have a cosmopolitan experience and was looking forward to her compulsory year abroad. She described some features that unified the liberal arts students at her old institution in the following way:

> 'I'm thinking of open-mindedness, especially because you come across so many different disciplines and ideas really – also international people throughout your degree – that it makes you realise that your point of view or your, yeah, your place where you're coming from is not the only one. So, I think that makes people maybe relatively more open-minded than those who don't study [the degree].'

This movement from cosmopolitanism to open-mindedness and back again can easily slip into ethical judgement, as *narrow*-mindedness is hardly a positive attribute. The opposite of cosmopolitanism ('parochialism') may be implicitly invoked as a negative feature of those who would *not* be interested in a liberal arts degree. This normative claim was made particularly explicitly, and straightforwardly, by post-war dean Tim. A language scholar who had himself lived in multiple countries, he had clear views on who might choose this type of study:

> 'Maybe the parents were in the army or maybe the diplomatic service, or people working abroad. They already – they'd been to another culture. It's – well you'd expect this from me, being bicultural, but it's just being able to see beyond the cliffs of Dover, basically. You know. Brexit! Don't talk to me about Brexit! I'm absolutely furious about Brexit. I mean, I think it's the worst possible thing that's ever happened to the UK. And these guys are the perfect Remainers, you know. I mean they are people who understand the value of different cultures, of thinking about other people, and people who are completely unlike yourself, in a different way. They accept that. It's the acceptance of otherness which I think is really valued in people who are really interested in the liberal arts.'

In painting this picture of who would be attracted to the liberal arts, Tim implies who it is that would *not* be interested. (If there are people who can see beyond the cliffs of Dover, then there must be others who cannot – something Tim elsewhere referred to as "little Englandism".) Due to the continual slippage between cosmopolitanism, progressiveness, open-mindedness and well-roundedness in the official liberal arts narrative, our sense of who would *not* want to study such degrees becomes negative in the extreme (Harpham, 2011): there aren't many who would willingly describe themselves as reactionary, narrow-minded and one-dimensional.

Interestingly, it was when Tim tried to bring nuance to his argument that the difference between those suited to a liberal arts degree and those who aren't was most strongly reinforced. Immediately after the "acceptance of otherness" that characterises his ideal student was noted, Tim went on to hedge: "On the whole. That doesn't mean that some of them might not be bigoted and might have rather weird political views. But the fact is that they're intellectually curious; they're open-minded. Generally speaking." Here, a division is made between the majority of students ("on the whole"; "generally speaking") who are characterised by curiosity and open-mindedness, and a minority who do not have these qualities. The mention of leaving the European Union, "weird political views" and bigotry in quick succession as what oppose the liberal arts mindset suggests a conflation between these three things, and although supporting any of them would not preclude someone from a degree like this, such people will be outliers.

Here, we are in the realms of what the website for one private institution's degree calls 'a diverse and like-minded student community': liberal arts students should be *alike* in their openness to difference, and such openness finds its limit when confronted with those regarded as 'closed' (Brown, 2006). This is one context in which the 'liberal' in liberal arts seems to take a cue from a certain version of political liberalism: its intolerance of 'intolerance' (Vora, 2019). And as we will see in Chapter 6, the complexity of the different ideas being conflated can easily lead to the casual inclusion of class judgements. Tim went on to note that, "typically, interdisciplinary-type students tend to be relatively high in their exam results, partly because a lot of them do IB – international baccalaureate – and are often people who are reasonably well travelled; they've been to private schools."

It's true that many students I spoke to expressed a desire for a cosmopolitan university experience and, in particular, for personal geographical mobility; often, as in Lotte's case, this meant international travel, though a desire to leave home towns within England, especially when this involved moving to large, diverse cities, was also common. This mobility is, however, often a strongly classed desire. Natasha, for instance, was a first-generation university student from England, now in her second year studying at an old institution. Initially describing herself as "quite middle-class", she later clarified that "I am in a sort of group of people where I don't get a big student loan, but I also am not really rich", explaining that she supported herself with a part-time job, rather than taking money from her parents. Enrolled on a liberal arts degree where study abroad was obligatory, Natasha had taken on a large number of extra hours at work in order to save for the upcoming travel. While she now felt that this had probably been unnecessary, she evocatively described the anxiety that the prospect of enforced cosmopolitanism (perhaps a species of Boltanski and Chiapello's [2005: 429] 'imposed self-fulfilment') had led her to:

> 'It almost put me off applying to [this university], although I know a lot of people applied because of it. So, a lot of people wanted that guaranteed year abroad because they're a lot more adventurous than I am. But I am not particularly adventurous; was very afraid of moving, like, as far as away as [this city] is from where I live, which is not that far. ... I'm still scared of the year abroad, but I think it's pushing me to be more of a rounded person, which was the point of it when they first – when they first mentioned it, and I asked, "Why? It's not relevant to my degree", they said, "We want you to become more rounded, global citizens", and at first, I was like, "Really? Come on!"'

Natasha weaved between hesitant claims that such mobility was unnecessary and much stronger self-flagellation for her lack of adventurousness. She was particularly concerned that she 'should' be pushing herself further, getting out of her comfort zone and the rest, even though moving halfway across the country to attend university wasn't exactly *in* her comfort zone. While the ways in which liberal arts degrees are promoted tend to present mobility as a necessary extension of cosmopolitanism and therefore an undoubtable good, for individual students, feelings of attachment to place may be more complicated (Claus et al, 2018), *especially* for first-generation students. Such students, often in quite gentle ways, seek to disentangle the blithely celebratory enmeshment of mobility with ethical goodness coming from institutions.

There are other ways in which students expressed their reservations about unbridled advocacy of cosmopolitanism, especially in relation to social class. This related to the fact that while the liberal arts did indeed seem to attract a diverse range of nationalities, the student body nonetheless remained homogeneous in class terms at many old and post-war institutions, being made up of a large number of students who had studied the international baccalaureate at international schools. Indeed, the appeal of such degrees seemed to be for an international *elite* in particular (as suggested by Tim's earlier mention of the children of diplomats and international businesspeople), leading to a lack of class diversity, despite the diversity of the cohort in general often being a key selling point. It is important to note that these concerns were only raised by students attending institutions with a reputation for attracting international elites across the board; however, the less privileged students at these institutions tended to say that the liberal arts degree was wont to exacerbate these problems.

Like Natasha earlier, such students tended to describe themselves as middle-class but distinguished themselves from some much more privileged students on their courses. Saad, for instance, was a British Asian, state-educated student from the north of England and had just completed his degree at an old institution in the south. He painted a clear picture of his sense of the liberal arts cohort, which, for him, related to gender and ethnicity, as well as nationality and class; on all four counts, he felt himself outside the norm:

> 'I always felt that it was – there weren't many people like me on the degree. In many ways. For example, a lot of them were international schoolers, quite a lot of French people, people who had done the IB. ... I was probably one of the few state school people on the degree from the UK. In terms of demographics: mostly female and mostly white. I think there weren't very many ethnic minorities. So, yeah, there were certain trends, and maybe that's why I found it harder to relate. Although there are people who are very nice and I did make friends with as well, I just felt that there were fewer on my degree programme compared with others.'

We need to be careful here, however, about allowing problems of class and ethnic diversity to effectively trump questions of nationality. This is an especial concern in a highly uneven higher education landscape where English-language degrees, particularly from internationally recognised universities, hold a great deal of cachet (Devos, 2003). That is to say, while class homogeneity is a problem for (many) liberal arts degrees, this should not blind us to the many ways in which UK students experience privilege over international ones, irrespective of class.

For example, Jessica had just completed her degree at the same old institution as Saad and was also state-educated (and, like Natasha, described herself as middle-class). She compared the behaviour of a clique of English public-school boys at her brother's Oxbridge college to that of a clique of French students on her own degree: in both cases, the students had attended an elite private school together, been "groomed" for prestigious universities and, once they got there, "just stuck with the people that they were used to". In one sense, these cases are indeed similar; however, the idea of people problematically 'sticking to their own' has very different political connotations around nationality than it does around class. To blame international students for not integrating is to take this purported behaviour to be an expression of privilege, as in the Oxbridge case. This is to take nationality (and language) out of the picture.

The idea of the cosmopolitan applicant, the cosmopolitan experience and the cosmopolitan graduate, then, while often presented as an unalloyed good in liberal arts promotional attempts, is a more complicated business when it comes to students' experiences. In particular, cosmopolitanism has a complex relationship with class, and while it is problematic to set these up in opposition (as in: 'liberal arts degrees promote classed ideas of cosmopolitanism, which less privileged students challenge'), we should be mindful that an unthinking conflation of mobility with open-mindedness, well-roundedness and the rest can have negative consequences for a range of students with different conceptions of belonging and home.

The knot of consumerism: choice, freedom and opportunity

In this final section of the chapter, we turn to what is perhaps one of the most commonly heard accusations against this generation of students: that they are consumerist. A number of claims are made about student identities in this regard but, in particular, that a focus on 'student satisfaction' is inherently opposed to intellectual understandings of education 'for its own sake' (Frunzaru et al, 2018) and that, specifically in the English fee regime, students have become both instrumentalist and petulant (Williams, 2012). This section attempts to offer a different way of understanding arguments made by students that are sometimes labelled 'consumerist', trying to show how a plurality of values are at play, including, crucially, highly *intellectual* concerns about rigour and *emotional* ones about a personal commitment to education. Rather than two poles of one scale, market concerns about value for money and inspirational ones about curriculum are thought of here as belonging to different normative orders As with simplistic stories about student cosmopolitanism and citizenship, ones about student consumerism likewise fail to get to grips with this complexity.

While in the last two sections, we were talking about *positive* accounts on websites (and from some senior academics), the aspect of identity being discussed here, consumerism, comes with a large amount of negative baggage. Institutions' promotional websites do not use the word 'consumerist'; instead, they tend to portray potential applicants as particularly concerned with individual choice. As against the idea that consumerist attitudes from students are what drives this focus on institutional websites, however, I argue that students (and junior academics) in fact seek to extricate intellectual and emotional values from financial ones (which they may also, albeit ambivalently, hold).

Institutions' promotional websites are keen to stress the liberal arts' connection to individualised conceptions of educational consumption. This often takes the form of a focus on individual choice and, in particular, stresses the possibility of cutting out those parts of a standard degree that the student may not be interested in so as to leave space for what they are: 'You're not stuck writing essays about something totally irrelevant to your goals' (website, post-war). (The use of glowing student testimonials on websites here can, as in other contexts, stretch the reader's credulity past breaking point: 'This wide range of subjects allows me to not only be able to build a degree tailored specifically to my interest, but I have never once been bored in any module I have taken!' [student testimonial, website, post-war].)

While, as I will go on to show, students themselves did not tend to make consumerist statements of this sort in interviews, they did report that some *academics* encouraged a you-said-we-did mentality. There were a number of instances given where liberal arts lecturers had elicited extensive feedback from students on an explicit understanding that the response would be swift. Here is just one example, where second-year student Natasha compared her experiences in the first year with those of the next cohort:

> '[The programme director] bought us coffee and cakes, sat us down in a sort of circle of ten and said, "Okay, what did you like about this [core] module and what didn't you like? Like, I can take it." And he edited it. So, when we've spoken to first years, they've said, "Oh, they're not doing this, but he said you did it last year", and we were – and that was in direct response to our feedback.'

On promotional websites, such amiability can tip over into desperation: 'It's an evolving programme and if you join us now you will be involved in the ongoing design of the programme – "What else do we need to add? What else will be cool to do?"' (website, old). My point is not that academics shouldn't solicit and act upon feedback from students (I've even been known to do this myself), but that solicitation is precisely what it is. To interpret this as consumerism *from students* is to invert the process and, indeed, the power. It is less you-said-we-did and more we-asked-you-answered.

In as much as consumerist views were expressed in interviews, this was generally very senior academics attributing consumerism to students. It also tended to relate to a specific notion of consumerism as connected to both student fees and employability; that is, that because students were paying large sums of money, their concern would necessarily be attaining well-paid jobs at the end. Post-war dean Tim, again, contrasted the market value of the liberal arts with that of 'mono-disciplines' like currently fashionable criminology:

> 'Will the criminology bubble burst? It's very difficult to say. When people see that they're not getting jobs any more, and you've got the TEF [national teaching assessment exercise], which shows, you know, what your job prospects are eventually. When people have a cold hard look. You know, when they're paying fifty thousand, fifty thousand in debt and they're having a cold hard look and they're thinking, "Is

this going to give me a job at the end?" And they see that criminology can't deliver the jobs.'[1]

Pro-vice chancellor Alan, a senior academic at a teaching-focused university with a very different student demographic, used the same reasoning to make the opposite point: "And that employability gain is obviously so much more dominant in the fee regime. So, any sort of instrumental approach to education kind of militates a bit against [the liberal arts], doesn't it?" Alan believes that for the largely first-generation, home students attending *his* institution, a direct relationship to one particular job is more valuable than the kind of interdisciplinary preparation for a range of futures that Tim expects students at his post-war institution to desire.

While Tim is explaining why the liberal arts may be popular, and Alan is explaining why they may not, they both understand students' reasoning processes as fully instrumentalist and, more specifically, as economically driven. What is missing from such accounts is an understanding that there is *more* to reason than instrumentalism (Sayer, 1999). Students may take a 'consumerist' approach that is nonetheless driven by their interest and passion (Nordensvärd, 2010): the buying of an opportunity, rather than a straightforward product. Students (and indeed most less senior academics) tended to give much more complex accounts of why the liberal arts are increasingly popular, and while tuition fees were certainly mentioned in this context, this was in far from unequivocal ways.

The closest I got to the kind of straightforward student consumerism outlined by deans Alan and Tim was when I interviewed students at a private institution. In this context, students were notably inclined to see their engagement in the interview as an opportunity to give feedback about what they did and did not like about their course, as opposed to the more personally reflective exercise it was taken to be by most other students. Third-year student Logan, for instance, reflected at length on how English liberal arts degrees might more compellingly market themselves to US students like himself, particularly focusing on the fact that English degrees are a year shorter, and therefore cheaper, than their US counterparts.

---

[1] It is worth noting that Tim's concentration on criminology here may relate to his perception of my own, connected, discipline of sociology. At various times during the interview, he turned the tables on me, subjecting my discipline to just the same kind of scrutiny that the interview was placing upon the liberal arts: "Sociology's an important part of the make-up of the faculty. And in my view should remain so, for at least the time being until something cataclysmic happens nationally with sociology. Which might never happen; hopefully never happen"; and "Sociology is a 70s' and 80s' discipline which a lot of people don't see as being as important, or useful, or fundamental as we did say during the 70s and 80s. I mean you know that: you're a sociologist."

The more explicitly consumerist discourse in this private context may be unsurprising, but it is important to note that there was significant ambivalence here too. Third-year student Johanna was a staunch advocate of private education in general and offered the most strongly consumerist views of all the student participants ("Should I say that directly? I'm not sure. But I feel like, yeah, I'm treated like a good client, if that makes sense"); yet, she was keen to temper this with a strong claim that she was not a consumer only and not treated as such by her lecturers: "I paid for this education here and I get some – the right platform off people. I get the right support and I feel that support is genuine. It's not a support that is bought; it's a support that's genuine."

One of the main contexts in which tuition fees and debt *were* introduced, across the student interviews, was in fact through an assertion that the money had been paid for an *opportunity to work hard*. This was exemplified by a pithy reflection from Jessica, completing her liberal arts degree at an old university: "I mean, I didn't come to uni and into 60 K of debt not to be challenged." In this often-expressed sentiment, students were far from absolving themselves of educational responsibility or asking to be spoon-fed; quite conversely, a passive or easy educational experience was considered a waste of money.

This is something akin to an effective use of gym membership: if we aren't active about it, the membership in itself will not help us to become fit. However, there seem to be some differences between how the gym analogy works for students and how academics tend to think about similar questions of autonomy, independence and hard work.

As academics, we often think of students' control over the use of their time as one of the important ways that higher education is not like school. Universities do indeed provide opportunities to learn, but this cannot be reduced to the number of contact hours provided. And, of course, students value control over their time too. Agathe was spending her third year on study abroad when we talked and compared the highly regimented and school-like structure of this experience with the autonomy she was granted at her post-war home institution:

> 'If you're not working, it's your problem. I mean, you're over 18 years old. You're just like – you decided to go to uni. If you decided not to work one week and to work another one, it's what you decided. So, we should be able to make those kind of decisions.'

Here, Agathe points to the importance of autonomy over time as a marker of adulthood. Indeed, this formulation of autonomous adulthood is central to how many students think about the value of a liberal arts degree, as well as higher education more generally.

What students often stressed, though, was the freedom to choose *how* to take up educational opportunities and, indeed, whether to take them up or not. Crucially, this included the right to make 'bad' choices, such as not turning up to class, writing an essay the night before the deadline or making curricular decisions that will be difficult to explain to future employers. Second-year student Mathilde reflected that some of her peers studying the liberal arts at her old university merely followed their personal caprices, rather than curating a logical pathway, as she had done: "So many students do anatomy, classics and design, and I don't see that going together. But, I mean, it's their choice."

By this logic, whether good or bad, choices can only be made meaningfully if there are a large number of opportunities to choose from. After all, gym membership is not just access to some equipment that we can choose to use or not, like an academic library. What about the personal trainer or the timetabled class? It would be a bit rich if the gym told us not only that we needed to stop being so dependent and just use the equipment ourselves, but also that this circumscribed set of options was actually what *enabled* our personal growth. The argument that a low number of contact hours facilitates a more responsible approach to time management was, for this reason, often experienced by students as just another form of paternalism ('Be autonomous when I tell you to be!'), if not a downright swizz.

It was when the educational opportunities themselves felt limited, then, that a particular type of consumerist narrative might emerge. Second-year student Konstantina, generally extremely positive about her experiences on a liberal arts degree at an old institution, was fairly typical in this regard:

> 'And actually, one of the things that everyone is complaining about, including me, is that we would like more contact hours. So, we have, like, what? Six a week? That's nothing; that's nothing. Eight hours of lectures per week? That's nothing. We're paying all that money. We'd rather have much more, and more modules.'

As we saw in Chapter 3, market-based ideas about personal choice in higher education have a strange relationship to individualism. On the one hand, they rest on the notion that individuals must be free to make different sorts of decisions (some 'good'; some 'bad'); yet, on the other, they rely on the assumption that everybody else is *like myself* in their desire to choose well (Boltanski and Thévenot, 2006). Students' hunger for maximum individual choice can even become universalised to *all* students. As Konstantina went on to say: "all students really want to do [liberal arts]. All of them. I've never met anyone who hasn't been really happy with the idea of choosing their own modules."

However, contra the focus on individual choice found on some liberal arts websites shown at the beginning of this section, nearly all liberal arts students do experience curricular constraints, either in terms of core modules, elective pathways, distribution requirements or a combination. Further, many students could in fact see the value in this, especially those who were nearing the end of their course. This is paradoxically a desire to choose *not to have choice*. As we saw earlier, student Marta strongly valued curricular coherence over caprice, and she had in fact chosen her liberal arts degree over other, similar courses precisely because of the built-in structure. Like other liberal arts students, she felt that her general enthusiasm for a very wide range of disciplines had the potential to lead her astray, and it was this structure that was allowing her to construct an interdisciplinary yet coherent degree.

This enthusiasm characteristic of liberal arts students is yet another layer to add to the picture of apparent student 'consumerism'. Keenness can be an important driver for the more active and intellectually driven opportunity optimisation I am describing here. Konstantina, who talked earlier about her desire for more modules, more contact hours and more opportunities to *work* in exchange for high tuition fees, again expresses very well the importance of intellectual enthusiasm in this context: "Like, I really want to learn. I wish I could study for ten years; there's so many modules I want to do. Honestly, so many. I love all of my modules so much; I always get so excited that I learnt so much. I want to learn more."

This is not to say that students never do the kind of more simplistic consumer talk alluded to by the two senior academics, Tim and Alan, earlier. Importantly, in my interviews with students, consumer rights might be invoked as an argument of last resort when other ways of framing a dispute had failed. This happened, in particular, when claims that liberal arts students could take more or less any module they wanted had proven to be incorrect. Not only do promotional websites tend not to dwell on such exciting matters as prerequisite constraints and timetable blocks, but, in practice, students were also sometimes rebuffed from optional modules simply because the offering departments were prioritising their own students. Since the institutions had strongly encouraged students to believe that they had a *right* to be accepted onto these modules, it is not terribly surprising that there is a whiff of consumerism about their protestations.

Third-year student Will, for example, echoed messaging coming directly from his post-war institution when he noted that "liberal arts literally have a mandate to do that kind of thing from the university. It was set up by the vice chancellor for those kind of things." Will is one student who was inclined to use the language of consumerism more broadly, yet he was clear that there is a difference between wanting to give feedback and expecting all requests to be acted upon wholesale: "Now they would ignore it when we would just say that we wanted the least work possible for the best grade possible." The blurring of this important distinction between 'you said' and 'we did' is one way that simplistic ideas about consumerist students can take hold in the academic imagination.

As teaching fellow Betka, working at the same post-war institution as dean Tim but with considerably more student contact, attested, the consumer rights narrative is heard, but she did not regard this as radically different, at heart, from what students have always said. Hearing what is meant by apparently consumerist ideas required, she thought, paying very close attention to students (Ahmed, 2015):

> 'But actually, to listen to what they're saying, it's just, "If you're a diligent teacher", or lecturer or administrator or anything. ... That is what it is. It's just the language is a little bit different. It seems more demanding, but actually, you know – I mean if they're asking something unreasonable, you can still say so, you know? Even if they are customers, you know?'

Since this language is available to them in the current fee regime – and is in fact encouraged by politicians, institutions and some, generally senior, academics – it would be surprising indeed if students never used it. Betka points out that this does not seem to mark, however, a radical break with other sorts of ways of speaking. Students want certain things from lecturers, just as lecturers want certain things from students (that they complete their reading, for instance). Sometimes, these requests will be met; sometimes they won't.

We have, then, travelled very far from the rather straightforward fostering of consumerist mentalities on some liberal arts websites and the common-sense views about tuition fees and student instrumentality suggested by some senior academics. In interviews with students and less senior lecturers and teaching fellows, the complex, ambivalent and context-dependent nature of student identities comes through strongly (Budd, 2018). And while some notion of consumer rights is part of this mix (especially in the context of disputes about access to modules and the subsequent justification for one's position in that dispute in an interview), this does not make it the fundamental truth of students' mindsets (Hughes et al, 2020).

Conclusion

In this chapter, I have tried to point towards some of the complexity of liberal arts students' identities and, in particular, how these depart from the simple stories that institutions and, at times, some senior academics may tell. The point is not that promotional websites don't, of course, have the space to get into lengthy philosophical conversations about complex plural value systems; it is that some of the *most* problematic ideas about student identity are being presented in extremely simple ways. Both class-riddled notions of citizenship and cosmopolitanism, and extremely simplistic notions of consumerism and instrumentality, do our actually existing students a great disservice. They also require super-human degrees of cloth-earedness. The chapter has not tried to show that these aspects of student identity are not indeed part of the mix, but rather that students themselves work hard to complicate such simplistic ideas.

As students show us, then, we need to move beyond the observation of a plurality of values within higher education, to address ourselves to questions of fairness (Giraud, 2019). Are all types of value system equally appropriate within educational considerations? Or, more practically, are there value systems that we would seek to exclude from education, or whose influence we would seek to limit? (The proviso that we may be unlikely to fully exclude them in practice is important but does not help us answer the question of whether we should make moves in that direction.) In Chapter 6, we will place front and centre those questions of social class and elitism that have been present in this chapter and before. We will ask how the liberal arts approach to education engages with one value system in particular: what Boltanski and Thévenot (2006) call 'domestic worth', meaning personal qualities like character, independence and flair. And we will also ask whether domestic worth is a *fair* thing to look for in particular educational settings.

6

Meritocracy and mass higher education: character, ease and educational intimacy

'Why don't we all do everything? People would be so much smarter.' (Konstantina, second-year student, old)

'It was capped at 20; it was always capped at 20. Because there was this understanding that they needed individual guidance and support. ... Also, the quality of students, you know. It's never going to recruit a hundred students, but for the very specific niche degree, we're doing really well.' (Hélène, programme director, post-war)

These two conceptualisations of the value of the liberal arts put forward by student Konstantina and academic Hélène suggest very different ways of thinking about who the liberal arts are for. For Konstantina, everyone should maintain a breadth of subjects. Hélène, on the other hand, expresses two sorts of reservation about this. First, she notes that the pedagogical and pastoral style best suited to the liberal arts favours a low student–staff ratio. Second, she suggests some kind of pay-off between the quality and quantity of students, such that the value of the specific *type* of students attracted to the liberal arts is thought to outweigh the value of a large number of students in general. She describes it as a "very specific niche degree", precisely not one likely to appeal to, or perhaps be suitable for, the majority of students.

This tension when it comes to advocacy for the liberal arts – considering it, often, to be an ideal type of education for all and yet somehow also only appropriate for a specific type of student – gets to the heart of a set of debates about elitism in a mass higher education system that will be the focus of this chapter. Here, the concept of massification is understood not only to mean a particular proportion of young people (say 40 per cent) accessing higher education, but also, more expansively, to refer to a general narrative of aspiration towards higher education for the majority (Scott, 2012) in a context where 97 per cent of new mothers want their children to attend university (Centre for Longitudinal Studies, 2010, cited in Scott, 2021). This context of massification creates tensions for institutions, which must weigh up competing pressures to recruit large numbers of students while trying to maintain league table positions. It also creates problems for students, battling inflationary pressures where they are told simultaneously that they must attain more qualifications to compete *and* that their qualifications are less and less valuable (Ainley, 2016a).

How do both institutions and students (particularly, for our interests here, elite institutions and more privileged students) respond to these pressures? In this chapter, I will argue that one response has been an increased folding of domestic values (Boltanski and Thévenot, 2006) into the educational sphere. By domestic values, I mean a concern with interpersonal relationships and with questions of character and personality when it comes to suggesting who higher education – and specifically non-vocational and general higher education of the liberal arts sort – is for.

This increased focus on domestic values is sometimes championed as a reversal of the depersonalisation said to lead from massification. It argues against the coldness of the purely civic test of ability (such as 'mere' exam results), putting forward the idea that education is about producing well-rounded individuals and not merely examination-fiends. We see the move towards domestic values in the recent drive for character education in schools, which focuses on qualities like grit and resilience. I argue that at the higher education level, we should see recent innovations, including the turn to the liberal arts, in this light. However, I do not argue that domestic values have *supplanted* civic ones of public education for as many as possible; rather, they are increasingly entangled.

The critical argument structuring this chapter is not that domestic values have no place in any educational context, but rather that close attention must be paid to when they are being invoked and to what ends. Specifically, I argue that interpersonal relationships and matters of personality are important in classrooms but should not be brought to bear on educational tests. While this may seem an obvious, if not banal, assertion, in this chapter, I seek to expand what is commonly thought of as an educational test.

There is a difference between saying that a particular educational form might develop certain character traits (like resilience or well-roundedness) in those who experience it, and saying that this educational form is best suited to those who *already have* such character traits. Expanding upon what is normally thought of as an educational test, I include any attempt, including the informal and implicit, to determine who is best suited to get into, get on within and successfully progress from any educational endeavour. This definition of the test goes well beyond questions of admissions and examinations, to ask what universities are implicitly 'testing for' in any number of small ways. This critical questioning of the values appropriate to a specific context is what distinguishes a pragmatic take on the complexity of values from a merely relativist or non-committal one (Jensen, 2018).

The chapter first addresses itself to the specific characteristics that liberal arts students are said to have, both on institutions' promotional websites and in the words of students themselves. I focus on one specific character trait – a kind of self-assured proactivity – and how this is conceptualised within liberal arts advocacy. I make a case, first, that this conceptualisation of the ideal liberal arts student can helpfully be understood in the context of the explicit turn to character education in schools, which has been the topic of much fruitful discussion (see, for example, Jerome and Kisby, 2019), and, second, that such conceptualisations are distinctly classed.

The next section attends to the question of whether domestic values are being *tested for* by the liberal arts. Here, we go beyond the description of positive character traits in the preceding section, to show that liberal arts advocacy in fact makes judgements about better and worse character. Taking the more expansive definition of an educational test sketched earlier, I argue that when institutions' promotional websites present their ideal student in terms of character, they thereby *test* for character, as they encourage some students to consider applying and others not to.

The notion of the independent, self-assured polymath explored so far, related to character traits like resilience and grit, is heavily classed. However, in the next section, we see such ideas become paradoxically entangled with seemingly opposed (but no less classed) conceptions of personal style and ease. Here, our focus is on small cohorts and interpersonal closeness, in short, what we might call educational intimacy. The fostering of such cosy smallness is one way that liberal arts degrees are conceptualised on promotional websites as resistant to the large, impersonal university, even while this intimate approach nearly always takes place in just such a large, impersonal institution. Students who had encountered both public and private education as part of their compulsory schooling, and who were now studying in a private university, said that liberal arts provision mirrored their positive experiences of small, private institutions and this was central to their affection for their degree. They entangled domestic ideas with civic ones quite happily. For some state-educated students, on the other hand, this atmosphere could prove cloying.

The next section asks, along with a number of students themselves, whether domestic considerations of interpersonal relations could impede fairness. That is to say, if domestic values are, on our new and expanded definition, being tested for by higher education institutions, is this a fair test? Rather than happily entangling civic and domestic values, some students made a conscious effort to disentangle notions of personal care (which they valued in the classroom) from civic tests. This section also gives some brief historical context to the fluctuating role of domestic values in education, stressing the primacy of context for determining the appropriateness of such values, as argued by students themselves.

Finally, we look at the relationship between character education and meritocracy, focusing on complex entanglements between 'natural ability' and 'hard work'. While educational intimacy relates to ideas of ease and comfort, the rigorous, independent spirit of the ideal liberal arts student relates to hard work and effort. As Michael Young (1958) could argue in the 1950s, this entanglement of the easy and the hard is central to how meritocracy is explained, as well as justified. However, this is an important, and rare, example where *none* of my interviewees noted a problem with an entanglement of values or sought to do any disentangling of their own. As such, I argue here, as well as in the subsequent Conclusion to the book as a whole, that this is an entanglement that educators must prioritise unpicking now.

The character of the liberal arts

One key focus in the literature on the burgeoning character education movement has been how education for character (often understood as self-motivation and grit) aligns with right-wing agendas that individualise social problems, locating the blame for social inequality on low aspiration and insufficient get-up-and-go; that is, on a deficiency of character. This alignment is not mere happenstance; rather, the character education movement has been explicitly developed and funded by right-wing organisations, as Kim Allen and Anna Bull (2018) have shown in their work on the role of US philanthropists in UK character education initiatives. Historically, character education can be linked to Victorian public schools, with their cult of the individual headteacher (Rothblatt, 1976), manliness (Collini, 1993) and the stiff upper lip – all designed to prepare the English upper classes for home and colonial rule (Sayer, 2020).

As critics point out, this deeply classed history can be read into current character education attempts. In 2015, for instance, then-education secretary Nicky Morgan launched a campaign to promote rugby union in state schools in order 'to instil character in disaffected and disadvantaged children' (Department for Education, 2015; see also Morgan, 2017) – an idea so baldly classed that it might have been passed up by the writers of *The Thick of It* as a little too on the nose. By focusing on such unabashed initiatives, however, we may miss the more subtle ways that character is not only said to be lacking among many young people, but also how they are being tested to see if they have it or not. Here, I wish to expand our understanding beyond what has been termed 'character education' in order to understand the focus within liberal arts advocacy not only on institutions' websites, but also among academics and students, on personal qualities like enthusiasm and well-roundedness (in addition to resilience, self-motivation and entrepreneurialism) as a turn to character. At the end of the section, we drill down into the specifics of one aspect of the ideal liberal arts student (the self-assurance to make one's own decisions) that exemplifies the highly classed nature of the turn to character.

In interviews with academics and students, as well as on institutions' promotional websites, confidence and initiative were presented as required even to consider such an unusual degree in the first place. Michael, for instance, worked as a liberal arts programme director. In the context of his modern university, which focuses on the traditional disciplines, he thought: "You have to be quite firm in your choice and quite kind of confident in your choice when others around you are taking PPE [philosophy, politics and economics] or history or English." Beyond this initial outlay of character, websites tend to stress that perseverance and independence of mind are required too in order to navigate the degree; and are, finally, an outcome of having studied the liberal arts. Thus, character is stressed for applicants, students and graduates alike: 'Throughout the programme, our students develop skills in academic resilience, initiative, and intellectual independence' (website, old); and 'Outside an educational context you realise the invaluable skills that [the degree] teaches you: proactivity, teamwork, determination, leadership, preservation, maturation, confidence' (student testimonial, website, old).

This self-directed personality type was also noted by students. Third-year student Josh reflected that at his old university, "you do get a certain sort of person on the degree programme. And I think that comes a lot from looking for a course, and also being on a course, where you have to take control of your own education."

In student interviews, the source of this sense of independence was sometimes thought to be a notably hands-off parenting style, where students had been encouraged to make their own choices from an early age. First-generation students, in particular, noted that their parents, while highly supportive and encouraging, tended to follow the students' own decisions when it came to education at a higher level (see also Burke, 2016). Finalist Agathe, for instance, had parents who were first- and second-generation migrants from North Africa and the Middle East. Neither had experienced university, and both adopted a hands-off parenting style when it came to educational decisions:

'So, they're not really educated, so all the decisions that I've made through my education over the years was mine, and they would just follow me. And this is what they tell me: "We don't know anything about it. We don't have the codes and the know, so whatever you choose is fine by us." So, they just trusted me.'

For more privileged students, whose parents had been to university, there had often been a similarly hands-off approach. The fact that the liberal arts was an unusual choice without any clear route to employment was not felt to be a problem as long as this was what they really wanted. Students felt that this was especially true when their parents had themselves felt parental pressure to take vocational or more conventional degrees. While Mathilde's parents back home in France, for instance, were both doctors:

> 'My mum, well, she was forced to do medicine. She wanted to be a home decorator. That was very free, and I knew I had options, and it was very up to me. So, I don't think it had an impact. I don't think it impacted me on not choosing literature [and instead taking the social-scientific stream at school]. I think it was me restricting myself, not from my parents.'

However, while this hands-off approach from university-educated parents may appear similar to that described by first-generation student Agathe, there are key differences. Agathe's parents feel they lack the competence to contribute to decision-making processes that they may wish they *could* assist with; by contrast, Mathilde's parents are making a conscious decision not to get involved. However, in addition, the more privileged students may in fact be experiencing a more subtly directional parenting, contributing to decision-making processes through dialogue in such ways that their influence remains implicit (Reay and Ball, 1998). This was exemplified by Bianca, involved in frequent conversations with her parents about which subjects to take on her liberal arts degree at a post-war university:

> 'I think, definitely, a lot of leaving me to make my own decisions. I think there's always a discussion going around with that – even now – about what I do at university sometimes, about what kind of subjects I would take. But it's not – it's just more of a kind of sounding board to what I think. It's not – I didn't feel like they told me what to do or anything like that. It was just kind of listening to what I want to take and then maybe offer a counter opinion, or saying kind of, "Have you considered this?" or "Have you done anything of that?" So, it was very, kind of, fluid and open, which I really appreciated actually.'

This soft, personal style of parenting does not, then, mean that the university-educated parents are not taking an active role in educational decision making (Bernstein, 1996). As we can see from this example of a highly valued independent-mindedness and its relationship to experienced parenting styles, then, ideas about the character of the ideal liberal arts student can be distinctly classed.

Testing for character: entangling the domestic with the civic

Although this is not true of all countries and cultures, in Britain Liberal Education has never been able to shake off its association with resistance to the twin advances of the natural sciences and the masses. (Scott, 2002: 71)

In this section, I go beyond a description of the ideal liberal arts student's character (for instance, as self-assured and proactive), to ask whether character is being *tested for* by the liberal arts. That is to say, are questions of character not only important for individual students and academics, but also suggestive of who ought to be applying for a liberal arts degree – and who shouldn't bother? To say that character is being tested for is to say that judgements of better and worse are being made; that is, that we are not in the realms of a neutral description of personality. Here, I draw on Boltanski and Thévenot's (2006) notion of domestic values, such as interpersonal relationships, trust, character and style, to argue that such notions of worth are indeed being transported into educational (that is, civic) tests. I also, however, show that both academics and students can be highly insightful about these problems because domestic values are not the hidden truth of the situation, but rather one set of values knotted in with others.

As Randall Collins (1979) could observe 45 years ago, greater access to higher levels of education appears to raise the educational stakes, rather than contributing significantly to social equality. For instance, as greater numbers of people attain first degrees, so greater numbers in turn seek out postgraduate qualifications in order to distinguish themselves on the job market. Patrick Ainley (2016a) offers the instructive image of young people running up a down escalator: they are told that they must attain ever-higher qualifications in order to compete, yet the very process of more people attaining those qualifications dilutes their value.

Increasingly, even some higher qualifications, such as a master's in business administration (MBA), become denigrated in this inflationary situation. Gerbrand Tholen (2017) characterises this as a move from traditional social closure to symbolic closure: rather than a physical monopolisation of opportunities because such opportunities are inherently limited (as when there were a very small number of university places), elites within symbolic closure monopolise the social meaning and value of different credentials that are now more widely available.

Importantly, such inflationary pressures do not just produce a drive for *more qualifications*. Purely civic tests, such as anonymised and depersonalised examinations, tend to favour those who have put more of their eggs more firmly in the educational basket: Bourdieu and Passeron's (1979) ultra-keen exam hound, rather than the more nonchalant dilettante. Crucially, it is the less socially privileged educational success stories who tend to fit this model of the exam hound. By contrast, more privileged students increasingly seek to set themselves apart via *extra*-educational criteria, rather than continuing to compete via the amassing of credentials. While this may mean, as we saw in Chapter 3, the take-up of extra-curricular activities, it can less obviously mean a drift towards domestic values in addition to civic ones in some educational tests; that is, a tendency to test for character traits in addition to academic aptitude.

There is a difference, of course, between saying that character is fostered as one moves through a degree and saying that it is (explicitly or implicitly) tested for in advance; that is, that character is a criterion upon which acceptance onto a degree may hang. One thing that makes some liberal arts degrees different from more conventional courses in the English context is that character is sometimes explicitly invoked as a consideration in selection. 'Mere' grades are contrasted with the well-roundedness that is sought out in appropriate applicants:

> Liberal arts at [this university] is a small, close-knit group of faculty and students, and we know how important it is to ensure that we don't just accept students with high marks. Rather, our students represent the most ambitious, energetic, independent, and creative university entrants, eager to work collaboratively to continually reshape the programme for themselves and subsequent generations of Liberal Arts students. (Website, post-war)

This focus can be even more acute when selection measures beyond the national Universities and Colleges Admissions Service application are used, such as interviews, entrance exams or additional personal statements. Quite explicitly here, character is being tested for; yet, the *criteria* upon which candidates might be assessed for character remain implicit, if not downright mystical: 'Our offers are not the result of some formula; this is a highly personal process' (website, post-war). Such vague principles are akin to what Brown and Hesketh (2004: 10), in their study of elite graduate recruitment processes, call 'the science of "gut feelings"'.

Relatedly, how students are assessed becomes unmoored from questions of content and directed towards ones of style. As one set of instructions for a liberal arts admissions assessment has it: 'The markers will be looking for examples of flair, linguistic accuracy and style, the ability to make interesting and relevant connections and links, and the ability to contextualise knowledge where appropriate, so there is nothing specific that you will need to revise before taking the test' (website, old). This description captures well a kind of intangible, but instantly recognisable, academic sprezzatura.[1]

Informality is a crucial feature of such a shift: as against the cold rigidity of civic tests, the domestic register stresses interpersonal warmth as a key criterion for getting into, getting on within and successfully moving on from

---

[1] I am grateful to Sivamohan Valluvan for teaching me this word.

the liberal arts. One website, for instance, describes networking evenings with prospective employers as very different from more formalised routes into graduate roles. These events 'allow our guests to identify students who they might want to consider for internships or permanent roles. Students can learn more about what companies do in a relaxed and informal context without the pressure that can go with feeling a need to "sell" yourself' (website, private).

Non-vocational higher education has long been considered well placed to provide the vague, desirable personal attributes of independence of mind, confidence and so on required of elite workers: Tholen et al's (2016) 'graduateness'. In the very competitive Civil Service Fast Stream, for instance, humanities graduates were the most recruited in 2016, while business studies saw one of the highest disparities between application and success rates (Institute for Government, 2018).

One institution's promotional website for the liberal arts links to an article from the BBC, which both describes the ideal journalist's attributes and notes which degrees are unlikely to foster such talents: 'qualities such as energy, enthusiasm, flair, imagination, passion, analytical skills, intellectual curiosity and a reluctance to accept things at face value. ... It is fair to say that many senior journalists are suspicious of media studies courses and doubt their relevance and value to a career in news' (Baker, 2012). It is not communicated here quite why a media studies degree would not produce the same qualities of graduateness as other courses in the humanities, and it's hard not to read this as an appeal for applicants with organisational fit in terms of their educational trajectory. In particular, this common-sense rejection of media studies can be seen as a rejection of the naivety that would lead someone to choose an applied degree containing the name of the job they hoped to attain in the title. As another university's liberal arts website puts it: 'What we're hearing from the really good employers is "We don't want students who've done Business Studies – we can teach them that"' (website, old).

A wide range of sociologists and others have shown that distinctions between more and less employable graduates should be understood in terms of employers' interpretations of nebulous concepts like talent (Brown and Hesketh, 2004) and organisational fit (Friedman and Laurison, 2019) – or even 'Googliness' (Ingram and Allen, 2019) – as much as the actual competence required to do particular jobs. In Glynne Williams's (2020) study of human resources practice, for instance, he found that psychometric tests were ranking applicants according to the working style of the top-performing new recruits *already employed* by the organisation, thus reproducing the existing organisational culture, rather than asking what attributes were required for the specific job in a more external and questioning fashion.

The privileging of degrees that are said to foster domestic values like 'flair' and 'passion', then, seems to require the denigration of their perceived opposite: training in specific skills, thought to both lead from and foster a kind of mindless pedantry. As Boltanski and Thévenot (2006: 247) observe in their discussion of a business manual on workplace 'style': 'The technician who is prisoner of his formal methods, the expert whose eye is riveted to charts, the manager obsessed with written instructions, all these are called into question for their very way of being, which denatures domestic worth.' This binary framing is certainly not new: 17th- and 18th-century scholars were well embroiled in disagreement about the respective values of specialism and polymathy. Jonathon Swift (1958: 232) brought out the point in stark relief when relating the allegory of the specialising spider and broadly educated bee in his 'Battle of the books':

> So that in short, the Question comes all to this; Whether is the nobler Being of the two, That which by a lazy Contemplation of four Inches round; by an over-weening Pride, which feeding and engendering on it self, turns all into Excrement and Venom; producing nothing at least, but Flybane and a Cobweb: Or That, by a universal Range, with long Search, much Study, true Judgement, and Distinction of Things, brings home Honey and Wax.

To say that character is tested for is to say that judgements are being made about *better and worse* character. This takes us beyond a mere description of personality, to a judgement on an individual's worth (Sayer, 2020).

Importantly, we see the *enmeshment* of civic notions of ability and competence with domestic ones about character and personality within liberal arts advocacy. The domestic has not supplanted the civic. In the context of the international baccalaureate as an ideal breeding ground for liberal arts students, for instance, senior academics often talked in interviews about students' grades at the same time as noting personal qualities like cosmopolitanism, not as separate attributes, but as one. Tim, for instance, told me about how he and others had got the liberal arts on the books at the post-war institution where he was dean. He stressed that the previous vice-chancellor:

> 'was very keen on pushing the general quality of the students up. So, I was able to argue to him, as an executive dean where we would be able to house something like liberal arts in our faculty, that it was very likely that we'd be pulling in some very high-quality students. Because, typically interdisciplinary-type students tend to be relatively high in their exam results, partly because a lot of them do IB: international baccalaureate. And are often people who are reasonably well-travelled; they've been to private schools – and [this university] wanted to actually bring in more private school students at the time, which was another argument for having liberal arts students because we assumed, and it

turned out reasonably correctly, that a largish number of them, of the applicants, would be likely to be independent schools.'

There is quite a lot going on in this quotation. There is a slippage between the intellectual attributes of the ideal liberal arts student and their social background, much starker here than elsewhere because of the remarkably candid admission that the university's strategies for prestige accrual included the targeting of private school students. (I do not mean to deny that many universities and, in particular, more elite ones than this post-war institution, are very clearly targeting private school pupils through formal and informal links, school visits and the rest. I only mean to note the starkness of the admission itself.) More specifically, there is a slippage from the ideal student's intellectual ability (measured by their academic attainment, or civic worth) to their cosmopolitanism (domestic worth) and on to their social background.

Here, it is almost as if the students are praised for their decision to take the international baccalaureate or to attend an international or even a private school; this decision indicates their intellectual openness. The use of the repeated word 'quality' here (as well as in the epigraph to this chapter) is doing a lot of work, seeming to signify something about students beyond their grades. Moreover, this invocation of the 'high-quality' student leaves unsaid what the quality of the students who normally come is.

For other, generally less senior, academics, this entanglement of domestic and civic values was noted and considered problematic. Nonetheless, it could be strategically useful in getting a liberal arts degree on the books, as Tim noted fairly uncritically earlier. Programme director Maria, working at an old institution, distinguished between what that nebulous and sinister entity, 'the university', wanted and her own feelings on the matter:

'And in order to get it through, you know, the rhetoric we adopted in the early stages – which, I mean, I wasn't very comfortable about at the time but, and which now we ditched – was that it was going to be a very sort of elite degree, that it was going to attract the best students. And that did help to get it on the books, for the university to be interested in it, 'cause we were saying, "You know, these are going to be students who are sort of polymathic, who don't want to specialise, who a lot of will have come from the baccalaureate. It will attract a certain kind of, you know, able student that we want more of at [this university]."'

Like Tim, Maria knows that she needs to use a certain language – to put on a certain hat or close her eyes to a particular reality – when talking to 'the university'. The elitist undertones (or, really, overtones) of the appeal to international baccalaureate students as the 'best' students are hardly lost on Maria, while she acknowledges their strategic use when talking to particular audiences. The acknowledgement of plurality here, as well as the attempt to remove domestic values from a context where they are not deemed appropriate (the elitist language was "ditched"), was an important feature of many interviews with both academics and students. This will be explored later in the chapter when I ask, along with interviewees, whether personalising the test in this way makes for a *fair* test.

Educational intimacy: the liberal arts and the question of scale

We have been exploring the ways in which liberal arts advocacy often not only describes, but also *tests* for, prospective students' ideal character. This is, then, a personalisation of the educational test or, as I am describing it here, an entanglement of civic and domestic values. This notion of personalisation has run throughout the book – when we thought about the idea of the bespoke, personally curated curriculum, for instance. Here, we turn to yet another way that liberal arts degrees are presented as personal: the idea of the *intimate* (that is, small, close and cosy) educational experience.

One specific feature of the US liberal arts tradition that is often drawn upon on institutions' promotional websites, especially those of old and post-war universities, is close personal attention to students and a focus on their individuality. Ideas about the small cohort, small seminars and a highly personalised experience are central to how the US liberal arts college is imagined as a 'community of learning' (Oakley, 1992), even if most students in England (and indeed many in the US) are experiencing the liberal arts in the context of much larger university structures than this: 'We know that a tight-knit, personal and intellectual *community* is key to your success' (website, post-war, emphasis in original).

Yet, this conceptualisation remains in tension with both market pressures that require even very elite universities to recruit large numbers of students and the disparate nature of students' subject choices and timetables, which make a sense of community difficult to achieve. This was a problem noted by many students, for instance, Rémi, finishing his final year at a large, old institution:

> 'We are spread into different majors, so it's quite hard in second and third year to meet each other. So, we're not – yeah, we don't fit. I think we don't feel really part of a core group, with a class like in high school, so it's really different. So, you meet a lot of people in some places, but, yeah, it's not, yeah, solidified.'

At better-resourced universities, much energy was put into creating a closer feeling of cohort and community, for instance, through dedicated communal space and social events. Now in her second year, student Natasha reflected on the conscious effort put in by staff to create a cohort identity, especially during induction week, which was compared to the experiences of friends studying elsewhere at her old university, who were left to their own devices much more:

> 'There are a lot of events that the liberal arts – both the liberal arts department ... and the liberal arts sort of group – or society – put on. So, they make sure there's a committee that put on events for everyone. We can all have a film night together. The department give us free wine; that's nice. And the first week – oh, and in introductory week – in sort of induction week even, we had, I think, a lot more time spent together than a lot of other [students] did. So, I know that a lot of people in induction week only had one or two lectures they had to go to, whereas we had about three full days.'

With very small cohorts, it might even be possible to house liberal arts students together in their first year in order to facilitate this sense of community.

While, as we have seen elsewhere in the book, promotional websites often stress that liberal arts degrees are inherently global and outward-facing, there is an invocation of smallness and cosiness here. Indeed, we even get these seemingly contradictory impulses in the same breath:

> A *personalised education* with one-to-one support.
> A *small campus* where staff and students get to know each other by name.
> A *global network* of students from more than 130 countries. (Website, private, emphases in original)

This idea that staff know students *by name* is an oft-repeated refrain on websites that invokes meaningful human interactions as central to university life: 'All the staff in Liberal Arts show a real sense of care for students – we are recognized by name as opposed to by number' (student testimonial, website, post-war). Implicitly or explicitly, the opposite of such care is also invoked, via the impersonality of the large lecture hall: 'There aren't huge lecture theatres with hundreds of students that you don't know, there tends to be really small classroom sizes with up to 15 people. This means that the learning environment is much more inviting and you actually get spoken to rather than spoken at' (student testimonial, website, post-war). Small class sizes (sometimes referencing the Oxbridge tutorial system) are, then, particularly valued because they lead to close personal relationships, with intellectual as well as other benefits: 'Over a term's tutorials, students work intensively with their tutors to develop their writing style and powers of organisation, enabling immense personal growth' (website, private).

The conscious effort put in to try to foster community was linked by many students to the holistic nature of the education itself, where the personal and the intellectual were not separated out. As Natasha, again, explained: "There's the very much sort of like tight-knit community, and there's the cultural events, so it feels like more of a holistic experience, if that makes sense. Like, the whole uni experience is liberal arts rather than being, 'Here's my degree', and then, 'Here's everything else.'"

A wide range of students valued this "intimate atmosphere", as first-year student Alina described her experiences at an old university. However, and while we should be mindful not to overstate this, those students studying at a private institution (all of whom had experienced some private education during compulsory schooling too) drew particular attention to the importance of small class sizes and teachers' personal investments in their students, often linking this to positive experiences with private education in general. In this context, the familiar distinction between small classes and large lectures was sometimes conflated with one between private and public universities in a relatively offhand manner. For finalist Logan, who came from the US and was thus familiar with a more mixed context of private and public institutions, "the fact that [this] is a private university with much smaller class size was definitely more appealing to me than other universities: public universities with a lecture size of a hundred-plus students and more, and the professor at the front".

In addition to linking the public–private distinction to class sizes, Logan also mentioned a sense that the financial element encouraged educators in private settings to invest personally in students' success, such that students would be driven to work harder:

> 'I think that the quality of education was so much better, and the main thing I'd say is, whether or not you wanted to do well in private education, they'd make sure that you did. They'd give you the right resources, they'd push you in the right direction, they'd start you off on the right track, and they'd get the parents involved.'

As we saw in Chapter 2 in relation to the international baccalaureate diploma, this highly directional teaching style is often understood by those students who have experienced it as more rigorous than the relatively hands-off approach of other educational forms (in the first case, A levels; in the second, public or state education). As we also saw in Chapter 2, this conflation of teaching intensity with teaching quality may be one reason that privately educated students sometimes struggle with the independent work required at university level (Bathmaker et al, 2016).

Sophie, also studying at a private university and also with experience of both public and private schooling at the compulsory level, made a series of connections between private education, small class sizes, the international baccalaureate and, crucially, ideas about the facilitation of individual choice.

Sophie: My favourite – I'd probably go back now if you asked me to – would be the IB programme. Just I – the style of education, the teacher–student sort of communication levels, interaction; I would say that really stood out to me above all else. But just – I just have experienced that in private schools: there tends to be higher attention paid to the desires of the students.
Kathryn: Right, okay.
Sophie: Which also falls into, you know, 'They want to do this one class and we can do that', and, 'If you want to do this–'. And it's just a little more free, I think, than when it's so regimented.

This is one of the many contested meanings of the 'liberal' in liberal arts, which casually connects quite elevated ideas about the freedom to learn with more prosaic ones about the freedom to *choose* (though for a problematisation of any simplistic association between the liberal arts and apparent student 'consumerism', see Chapter 5). Domestic values of interpersonal care are entangled with market notions of choice in quite an offhand way here.

On the other hand, some less privileged students, who had not experienced private schooling and who attended public universities, sought to disentangle domestic values of intimacy (which they appreciated in other contexts) from education. Where students had already experienced significant independent study, especially while taking A levels at comprehensive schools, the idea of a close 'community of learning' didn't always appeal – in particular, where this entailed living in close quarters, and even dining, with peers. For third-year student Jessica, the decision to study at a large university in a big city was influenced by her brother's experiences in an Oxbridge college: "I didn't want that. I didn't want to be catered for; I didn't want to feel like I was in a big boarding".

While the educational intimacy of the liberal arts and, in particular, small class sizes, is a feature thought to appeal to many students, higher education institutions are simultaneously contending with ever-increasing market pressures which mean that even very elite universities must focus on recruiting more students. For universities with elite aspirations, liberal arts degrees can be positioned as a 'premium product' allowing them to compete with some very prestigious institutions and even to raise their entry tariff, which is one factor taken into account in league tables. Educational intimacy clearly feeds into this idea of being an elite offering; yet, simultaneously, those advocating for the liberal arts must convince management that recruitment will be high.

Tim explained this in the context of the post-war university where he had been dean. This is an institution that had taken a very strategic approach to rising up the rankings in recent years, with notable success. Tim described a careful balancing act between competing institutional drives to maintain student recruitment while raising the entry tariff: "And the four deans, really, what we were trying to think about was how we were going to be able to improve the grades without actually damaging our market. So, we had, you know, we had a very carefully planned campaign over three years to start raising the grades." These pressures are not alien to more prestigious universities either, and there can be a quite acute desire here not to be *seen* to be diluting the brand by allowing in more students, as programme director Maria told me:

> 'I mean, my sense is that across the whole sector, people are taking students with lower grades than the tariff because it's become such a competitive market. [This university] is very self-conscious about not wanting explicitly – I mean, like so many places, do you know what I mean? We don't give unconditional offers or anything like that, like some places do.'

The image of a highly selective course is important for some institutions' offer, but the reality can again be rather different on the ground when pressures to recruit are felt. Third-year student Asif had applied to a liberal arts course that makes much of its highly selective and personalised admissions process before eventually choosing a different institution. Having attended an admissions interview, he recounted that "they sent me an email afterwards explaining like, 'Oh yeah, you're the perfect candidate for this.' They seemed to want me more than I – obviously I wanted to go but …".

It is of course possible to think of the turn to the liberal arts as a critique of the forces of marketisation that have seen student numbers rise and student well-being fall since the introduction of top-up fees and the replacement of student grants with loans in the late 1990s. In resistance to the kind of pile-'em-high, economy-of-scale, cookie-cutter degree that critics say has come to prominence over the last 25 years, the turn to the liberal arts asks us to slow down, to treat our students as individuals and to wonder whether there is more to education than getting the maximum number of people through the gates. As programme director Hélène points out in the epigraph to this chapter, there is value in the degree even if "it's never going to recruit a hundred students".

However, Hélène also related this to what she at various times referred to as the 'quality' of the students it *did* recruit: "it was quite a marked difference from the norm of students we get. Even, you know, being a good university. I did interview a student from Eton at some point." Thus, while notions of smallness, closeness and intimacy may on one level offer a refreshing shift from the fast pace and apparent impersonality of the Brobdingnagian modern university, it would be troublesome indeed to suggest that nostalgia for a past before massification was straightforwardly progressive. Such nostalgia remains tied up with images of an ideal university before students of a different 'quality' began to seek out a place in higher education (Meyerhoff and Noterman, 2019).

Character, closeness and the question of fairness

The idea of the impersonal behemoth of a university has come to be something of a bogeyman in some quarters. In this context, as we've seen, there is often a distinction made between knowing students' names and treating them as a number, with the former obviously good and the latter obviously bad. Yet, I will argue here that treating students in depersonalised ways, indeed, as numbers, is a crucial mechanism for ensuring fairness in higher education when it comes to making assessments. As throughout the chapter, here, I mean assessment in an expansive sense, going beyond formal examination, to encompass the ways in which universities test for competence and fit, including not only admissions processes, but also all the informal mechanisms by which institutions and those who work in them send messages about their ideal students; that is, about who will and who will not fit in a particular educational context. While a personalised approach to students is of course desirable in the classroom, these broader personalisations, so that individual character traits are considered relevant when thinking about ideal students, are problematic.

The idea of treating students like numbers can be traced back to a set of 18th- and 19th-century concerns to separate out public from private life. As against a domestic register where private considerations (for instance, personal relationships, reputation or ideas about character) had been considered quite legitimately brought to bear on questions of public assessment or appointment to office, with the extension of the franchise and the rise of liberal-democratic ideas, this intermingling of the private and public came to be seen as suspect (Boltanski and Thévenot, 2006).

Ansgar Allen (2014) offers two instructive illustrations of these (incomplete and contested) historical shifts. First, over the course of the 18th century, examinations at Cambridge moved from the oral disputation, to a written examination where questions were read out by examiners, to finally a written paper. In this move from the spoken to the written, the individual personal presence of the student, and finally the examiner too, is removed, so that assessment can be conducted in as depersonalised a way as possible. In a more outlandish example, Allen recounts Jeremy Bentham's (1983, cited in Allen, 2014) proposal for an educational test, which should proceed in the following rather complex fashion: first, for each subject, a comprehensive book should be produced with all possible questions and their answers; a random selection of these questions would then be drawn by lot; to each question would correspond a ticket, and the randomly selected tickets should be placed inside a cylindrical tombola drum; a cloth with a slit the size of a child's hand should be placed over the box; and finally a child should be provided to draw the tickets, their inherent innocence thought to ward against corruption.

As Allen notes, the peculiar level of detail here suggests that the ideas of depersonalisation and fairness being invoked were at this stage both new and contested. The 19th-century Oxford academic Mark Pattison, for example, was highly critical of what he regarded as a move away from the importance of a personal love of learning, despite being simultaneously disparaging of John Henry Newman's ideas about the role of the teacher in 'character building', which were also in circulation at the time (Jones, 2007). Clearly, personalised modes of assessment never did disappear, as we can see, for instance, in the continued use of admissions interviews at both Oxford and Cambridge. Rather, there has been a complex history of more humanistic ideas about highly personalised forms of education moving into and out of fashion over the centuries (Kimball, 1986).

As I argued earlier, it is too simplistic to understand calls for a more personal form of education as either inherently progressive (because they critique forces of marketisation and depersonalisation) or inherently regressive (because they are nostalgic for a time before massification). Rather, I argue that whether we should treat students like numbers depends upon the context (Walzer, 1983): impersonality is problematic in the classroom but not when making assessments about who is best suited to this or that type of education.

This concern with educational context came out in interviews. Junior academics and students sometimes conveyed doubts that academic tests were properly civic (that is, tests of ability), rather than tests of character. Teaching fellow Betka noted that liberal arts students seemed to perform better in oral presentations than in their written work and that this was a striking difference from single-subject students she taught at the same postwar university. When I asked why she thought that liberal arts students were good at presentations, she was unsure but noted some possibilities: "I don't actually know. Baccalaureate? Education? Background? Confidence? Not all confident, but even those who are not confident are good presenters, overall. I literally don't think I had – maybe I had a bad presentation. One." Here, Betka offers a range of explanations in quick succession, suggesting both civic and domestic values.

Some students who strongly valued intimacy in the way they were taught did *not* want such personal considerations to affect how they were ultimately judged by teachers. Finalist Joe reflected on his three years at a private institution and criticised how the very intimacy of the liberal arts classroom meant that teachers would know whose work they were marking even in the context of formally anonymised assessments. He sought to disentangle the personal from the impersonal:

> 'So, I didn't really like that aspect of having to, not having to suck up to the lecturers, but *be there*, so that they see you and they know you, so that when they do their paper, they can give you better grades. I think that happens a lot in liberal arts because the classes are really small. So, then they notice when you're not there. Whereas if it was like – if I went to [a public university] or something, to a massive lecture hall, they wouldn't be able to know who you are or anything like that.' (Original emphasis)

In this instance, the 'massive lecture hall', a symbol of the depersonalisations of mass higher education on promotional websites, is a guarantor of fairness.

First-year student Veronika similarly reflected on the unfairness of teacher preferences contaminating assessment in her earlier school experiences:

> 'Yes, I was a good student, but I kind of cheated. Because I was showing myself as a very proactive student, but because of the way Italian assessments work, you're not really – let's just say that they're not anonymised, so if you show to the teacher that you're keen on learning in the first few months, you're kind of fine for the rest of the year.'

Whether they believe they win by this personalisation of the test (as in Veronika's case) or they believe they lose (as in Joe's), students express concern that values that should be irrelevant to the test are being unjustly transported in from other spheres. Given that they express this concern even where personalisation works in their own favour, it does not seem right to characterise such fairness-speak as a mere cover for self-interest. It would also not be true to suggest that students extend their reservations about personalisation to all educational contexts, such as classroom interactions. In the same way that, as academics, we separate out those decisions requiring personalisation and, for want of a better word, humanity (such as mitigation for personal circumstances) from those requiring depersonalisation, if not, one hopes, *in*humanity (such as the application of those decisions to now-anonymised student marks), so students come to contextually appropriate judgements about the role that personality or character should take in different aspects of university life.

Beyond these concerns about formal assessment, a number of students (especially those from less elite backgrounds, or who had taken a more circuitous route to the liberal arts) recognised that there were other ways that prospective applicants were being tested. Similar to their thoughts about educational intimacy outlined earlier, less privileged students who had attended comprehensive schools, like Jessica, also tended to be more resistant to the moral timbre that ability and polymathy are given in some versions of the liberal arts story, where the civic value of high grades becomes attached to domestic ideas about being somehow 'the best'. While critical of her own institution in this regard, Jessica told me:

> 'To be perfectly honest, I was more put off by the people at [another old university] because they – in their – certainly when I applied, in the prospectus for liberal arts, it said, "A degree for the elite." I was horrified. It was just a big "no" from me. Just because you're capable of doing more than one subject doesn't make you better than everyone else.'

In instances like this, people involved in the liberal arts question what it is that is being tested and open their eyes to the possibility that it is an inappropriate worth.

The knot of meritocracy: intelligence plus effort, still

Earlier in this chapter, we came across Bourdieu and Passeron's (1979) schematisation of two types of educational success: the exam hound and the dilettante. On one level, such a binary schema might help us understand a number of things about some liberal arts talk, including the denigration of specialisation as pedantry. However, while originally formulated as two fundamentally opposed (and of course heavily classed) educational identities, in this final section, I explore how the two are entangled within liberal arts advocacy. That is to say, the ideal liberal arts student is at once presented as naturally able (like the suave, polymathic dilettante) *and* as a hard worker (like the ultra-keen exam hound).

Here, we examine the specific mechanisms by which domestic values are entangled with civic worth, through the meritocratic formula of merit = intelligence + effort (Young, 1958). It is the entanglement of the easy (talent) with the hard (industriousness) that gives the rewards that accrue to the generally educated the ring of fairness. Furthermore, since this is an important, and rare, instance where none of my interviewees problematised the entanglement, or sought to disentangle it, I argue here, as well as in the Conclusion to the whole book, that it is a key area for critical educators to focus on now.

When it comes to notions of intellectual ability, there is of course a long history of associating non-vocational education with higher intelligence, and in the case of the liberal arts, this is compounded by an implicit link between polymathy and ability too. Institutions' promotional websites casually refer to this association between the liberal arts and intelligence: 'I don't think my experience is a unique one because the vast majority of my fellow [liberal arts] cohort also achieved a First in their degree' (student testimonial, website, old). A number of students, like second-year Mathilde, specifically discussed having been bored at school, being ignored by teachers because they seemed able to achieve academically without much prompting:

> 'I was a very good student but not that interested. I would usually either make these friendship bracelets – you know, bracelets – under the table, and the teacher wouldn't say anything, or write my own notebooks; things like that. But I still had good grades, so they just let me do whatever.'

Rather than being discussed separately, moral ideas about character (for instance, notions of drive, resilience or self-motivation that we encountered earlier) are often tied in to notions of ability in subtle ways on promotional websites: 'Our students are unquenchably curious and of the highest calibre' (website, old); and '[The degree] appeals to highly qualified, self-motivated, and independent-minded students' (website, old). Since ability is casually tied in to positively framed personality traits, intellectual qualities are gifted with a moral timbre without this being made explicit.

The domestic register often naturalises differences, as if personal qualities were in individuals from birth, and websites may casually allude to 'the best' or 'brightest' students as if such terms were uncontested: 'It goes without saying that this highly challenging and innovative course attracts the brightest individuals' (student testimonial, website, old); and '[Liberal arts] students are, by nature, dynamic, busy people with lots of interests both within and outside the classroom' (website, old). In this appeal to what is already, and naturally, there and to be taken for granted, websites suggest that we can (with ease) select for natural qualities that already exist in individuals (Turner, 1960). This is something akin to Thomas Jefferson and other early-modern Americans' hopes that a liberal education should contribute to a natural (rather than a hereditary) aristocracy of the best and the brightest (Zakaria, 2015).

Some students suggested self-conceptions along the lines of natural brightness too. Will, who had just completed his liberal arts degree at a post-war institution, described himself as a "lazy shit" and went on to explain: "Quite lazy would have been the easy way to describe me academically. I'd sort of just float in, float out and get away with it. This has always been true." In this description of floating in and out of rooms, Will is similar to some students in Rubén Gaztambide-Fernández's (2011) study, who stressed the importance of confident "bullshitting" when they had failed to prepare for class at their elite school.

However, Will went on to explain that he had progressed from this "laziness" over the course of his university career:

> 'But I realised there will be things that I want to do, be it hobbies or goals or a career, where it will not be an issue of just being naturally bright and walking into a room. It will be an issue of how much I'm actually willing to strive to make something a success.'

In this reflective account, Will describes the need to supplement natural ability with something else: hard work. This notion of hard work, linked to favoured character traits discussed at the beginning of this chapter, such as grit and perseverance, seems to be in sharp distinction to the breezy ease of domestic worth. Yet, it is often found in close proximity to it. In the following, second-year student Ellie weaves between the natural and the worked-for when discussing the difficulties of negotiating multiple disciplines:

> 'I think that possibly the nature of the fact that students who are selected for liberal arts programmes means that they're people who are normally people that can pick things up quite quickly and can kind of keep up with the work and are willing to put in a little bit of extra work. If there's concepts that they haven't possibly understood or they haven't been taught previously, they'll do the extra work that's necessary to keep up with the others.'

Liberal arts students have a "nature" that is "selected" for, and they can "pick things up quite quickly". But they are also "willing" to "do the extra work". They *can* keep up with the work, but they *will* put in the work to do so.

While the idea that students can do the work *easily* seems to be in contradiction with the idea that they will have to work *hard* (the formulation is almost that liberal arts students find it easy to do work that they find hard), this tension is in fact central to the meritocratic formula first articulated by Michael Young (1958) as talent plus hard work. Competences like intellectual agility are said to simultaneously inhere in certain individuals and not others, *and* to be potentials that must be worked upon. This is what Ansgar Allen (2014) calls 'fluid' rather than 'mechanistic' meritocracy, where the 'correct' social order is thought to be a matter of contestation and effort, rather than a natural hierarchy of gifts and abilities merely waiting to be discovered. Talent is innate, yet it must be activated (Sardoč and Deželan, 2021): premier league footballers are thought to have innate talent, yet this talent has normally been worked on intensively in football academies from a young age. Historically, the shift from mechanistic to fluid conceptions of meritocracy marked a moral distinction between the hard-working, aspirational middle class and a decadent and complacent aristocracy (Hartmann, 2007). There is a complex relationship, then, between talent, hard work and deservedness in contemporary meritocracy (Ye and Nylander, 2021).

This conception of talent as something that must be activated by character is crucial for making meritocracy resonate with fairness. Rewarding innate talent alone is hard to justify (why should I be punished for something I can do nothing about?), but notions of aspiration and hard work, knotted in with beliefs about talent, soften the edges of brute nature as the criterion for reward. And the belief that the *capacity* for hard work is universally and evenly distributed (rather than being, say, an innate property of which some people have more or less) is paradoxically the very condition that allows a social hierarchy of more and less worthy people to emerge (Boltanski and Thévenot, 2006). Precisely because everybody is thought to be equally capable of hard work, the extent to which they choose to exercise that capability becomes a legitimate criterion upon which to reward (or to punish).

Conclusion

In this chapter, I have argued not that educational intimacy, interpersonal affinities and a concern with character are always inappropriate in educational settings, but rather that educational tests should be considered differently from other sorts of educational encounters. Ideas about the small cohort as a 'community of learning', for instance, at first blush appear as undoubtable goods. Yet, such an image appealed much more to privately educated students than to others in my interviews. Thus, by invoking such cosiness, we encourage certain students to think of themselves as prospective liberal arts students and discourage others from doing so. This is, then, an educational test. By expanding the definition of the test to mean not only those moments at which formal assessments are made, but also any message that is sent to both applicants and students about how to get into, get on within and get out of a liberal arts degree successfully, it can be shown that such courses are particularly inclined to test for character.

The point here is, though, quite different from one that would argue that educators and students are blind to the class inequalities tied up with ideas about ability, polymathy and 'the best' (see, for example, Bourdieu, 1988; for further discussion, see also Telling, 2020). People are not blind to this injustice, but rather open and close their eyes to it depending on the situation (Thévenot, 2014): in order to appeal to senior managers and get a liberal arts degree on the books, eyes may be closed; yet, in the context of a research interview, something rather different happens.

However, in the final section of this chapter, we turned to a knot that was unusual, in that no one seemed to challenge or unpick it within interviews.

This is the entanglement of hard work and talent within meritocracy, and I suggest that this *lack* of critique indicates that it is a particularly important issue for critical educationalists to focus on today. This argument will be picked up at length in the next chapter, which concludes the book as a whole.

Conclusion

On the one hand, and as its advocates often claim, there seems to be a particular timeliness to the liberal arts approach that would explain its increasing popularity, both in England and globally. On the other hand, we might just as well expect to see a move towards more technical and specialist education (Boyle, 2019), and indeed we do see that move at the same time; for instance, in the long-touted T level technical qualifications. I have tried to argue that the liberal arts do not present some inevitable direction of travel for English higher education, but rather constitute a much more complex mess of values that, by virtue of its very messiness, is able to *appear* as an inevitability and thus as the best imaginable form of education, rather than one among others.

Since the liberal arts approach is advocated as simultaneously the best preparation for modern work, as the most prized sort of education for the intellectual, as a personally curated degree for the world's individuals, as training in character, mind and soul – that is, because it is presented as the best preparation for work, leisure and life in general – it is the *entanglement* of these values that makes it possible to make hyperbolic yet vague claims for this as the best form of education in every context. It is also a brief hop from the idea that this is the best imaginable sort of education to the belief that it attracts the best sort of applicants and produces the best sort of graduates.

This conclusion begins with a discussion of plural values as at the heart of higher education today. Seeking to move beyond notions of *unveiling* within the critical sociology of education, which posit a fundamental truth (the reproduction of inequality) at the centre of educational encounters, masked by a cloak of legitimacy, this account stresses instead the idea of opening and closing one's eyes to different sorts of values, depending on what one is trying to do. Importantly, the students and academics I interviewed were themselves in the business of trying to unpack, and critique, what was happening in different educational contexts. This is a very significant difference between what individuals think about the liberal arts and how they are presented on institutions' promotional websites.

Far from being equally available, however, I argue that the complexity of an individual's insight about these questions is in inverse relation to their power (junior academics being more insightful than senior academics, for instance). This approach raises both ethical and practical issues about the nature of research interviews, which will be addressed in the following section. Finally, I make a last substantive claim: that the attention to plurality that has structured the whole book can lead us towards a potentially fruitful critique of meritocracy.

Plural values and the liberal arts knot

A key argument of this book has been that there are plural values at play in English higher education today and that the turn towards the liberal arts can be used as a lens to bring this plurality into focus. These values help those who study and work in universities to make sense of what goes on there and to make meaningful and justifiable decisions about how to act. I have argued that higher education is characterised by complex entanglements and compromises between these different values, and that claims that market values have taken over (as in critiques of the marketised university, the student as consumer or neoliberal education) miss much of this complexity (Gibson-Graham, 2006).

The pragmatic approach developed by Boltanski and colleagues has formed a loose grounding for this analysis. However, these ideas have, in the past, indeed been used by others to identify a near-universal neoliberal ideology. This is especially so when *The New Spirit of Capitalism* is taken to be the pinnacle of Boltanski's thought, rather than placed within the context of a large and developing body of work. However, even within that book, Boltanski and Chiapello (2005: 487) do not argue that what others call 'neoliberalism' is ever the only game in town:

> Perhaps these tendencies [towards capital accumulation] would be unbounded if human beings knew only one kind of goods and only one way of attaining them. But one-dimensional individuals of this variety – close to the fiction of *Homo oeconomicus* – would not grow indignant at anything, would have no compassion for anyone, or any critical spirit. There would no longer be anything distinctively human about them.

I argue that it is not helpful to think of different national higher education systems at different points in time as placed somewhere on a single-axis scale with 'completely marketised' on one end and 'completely for its own sake' on the other. Rather, if we think of these two extremes as actually existing on two *qualitatively* different scales – one relating to market values and one to inspirational values – we are able to get to a more complex picture more accurately reflecting the messiness of higher education as it is actually experienced (Oldenhof et al, 2013).

People rely on, and appeal to, different value systems depending on what they are trying to do, rather than carrying one perennial value system around with them as the fundamental core of their being, which may then become unfortunately compromised with other value systems, making such people hypocrites, or worse. Taking a pragmatic view, people are certainly strategic, but not in the sense of insincere or duplicitous. A senior academic may make a case to their manager for more resources for their department using terms that they would not use when out for a drink with colleagues from their discipline, but this does not make the second encounter more honest than the first (or indeed vice versa).

To use Bernard Lahire's (2011) helpful metaphor, it is more correct to describe a sugar cube as dissolv*ing* in water, rather than as *having* solubility as some eternal property regardless of context. This shifts our focus away from solubility, the noun (which encourages us to think in terms of inherent and enduring properties that the sugar cube carries around from place to place), and towards dissolving, the verb (which leads us to think of properties as existing in the interaction between object and environment).

As for sugar cubes, so for people: agreeing and disagreeing, speaking cynically or idealistically, are actions that we do or don't do in different situations, and while we can frame them as nouns (disagreement; cynicism), to do so is to give them a timeless quality. The research interview itself is a situation where participants may agree or disagree, speak cynically or idealistically, or put on different 'hats'. Merely having a particular set of values doesn't actually tell you what to do in any given situation; rather, this is a matter of dispute, negotiation and compromise (Fassin, 2013). Faced with a complex decision to make, to which a variety of value systems may be brought to bear, and rarely presented with a perfect answer, actors 'attempt to act ethically in unethical circumstances' (James, 2015: 105). And among all this, they must also act in ways that are likely to be perceived as ethical *to others*, placing limits on live options.

Liberal arts degrees prove especially helpful for observing some of these tensions, value struggles and compromises. The strange word 'liberal' has so many meanings, and arguing that what it *really* means is 'liberating' (or 'wide-ranging' or 'elitist' or 'egalitarian' or whatever) is never completely successful in shaking off the associations of its many other denotations.

For instance, the liberal arts often struggle to shake off their connection with liberalism as political project. But this connection is not a misunderstanding; rather, it is part of the overall messiness of the education's history. One manifestation of this is in competing conceptions of purpose. As Bruce Kimball (1986) has argued, the purpose of a liberal education might be thought of in terms of: a good, general education for all; for each according to their individual interests; or as the education to which all should aspire. It is not coincidental that these three types of purpose for the liberal arts mirror broader tensions within political liberalism between egalitarianism, individualism and elitism. As Kimball has also shown, ideas about preparation for leadership and the gentlemanly virtues rub up against ones of unencumbered intellectual exploration within liberal arts advocacy – sometimes comfortably; sometimes less so. These ideas come in and out of fashion and become compromised together in different ways, for instance, in the influence of both Oxbridge collegiate culture and the German research university in the development of the US liberal arts tradition.

Importantly, it is in *speech* where these complex entanglements best reveal themselves. In his work, Luc Boltanski has tended to focus on the written word for a number of reasons, including ethical ones, and in *On Justification*, Boltanski and Thévenot (2006) deliberately choose texts to analyse that exemplify one particular order of worth (such as the domestic or the civic). Each order is examined in turn, and while this by no means stops the authors from examining plurality (indeed, that is the whole focus of the book), nor compromises between value systems, it nonetheless can have a purifying effect. By this, I mean that just as *The New Spirit of Capitalism* can be read in simplistic ways, leading to analyses that foreground market values above all else, so a focus on different orders of worth *in turn* can neaten up the complexity of the situation. Instead, each chapter in this book has focused on a particular entanglement of values, an animating paradox or a knot as its smallest unit. Here, by allowing the spoken word to rub up against the written, the plurality, ambivalence and subtlety of people's accounts is shown in stark relief against more simplistic and celebratory written stories. This is also because of what I have called the 'hierarchy of ambivalence': the tendency for the spoken word to be more ambivalent and complex than the written, just as first-generation students tend to be more insightful about complexity than more privileged students or junior academics than their senior counterparts.

How ethical is it, though, to put plurality at the heart of interviewing when participants may quite reasonably take it that they are being asked questions about their fundamentally true beliefs, or indeed about their objectively true experiences (Hammersley, 2013)? More than one senior academic declined my invitation to participate in the research on the grounds that I had 'already spoken to Peter' and thus there was nothing more I could glean by conducting an interview with *them* on the history of the same degree. This may be a polite way for a busy person to say, 'I haven't got time', but it is also clearly saying that such an interview would be a waste of *my* time. For my purposes, on the other hand, whether I have already spoken to Peter makes no difference to my wanting to speak to Paul. It will be helpful, then, to turn next to some methodological reflections on plurality and interviewing.

Entering a dispute: plurality in the interview

Research interviews are a particular type of social encounter that encourage us to reflect on what we have done and, crucially, why we did it; that is, they easily take a highly reflective, and often justificatory, turn. Starting with rather prosaic questions about how the degree began, or which modules one is taking, it is a short hop to a discussion of whether a liberal arts degree would be right for this or that type of student, or whether a liberal arts degree is a good type of education. And from tests of truth like this, we easily find ourselves in a higher register still: how do we make judgements about our students? Should we be judging them at all? What does it mean to call an education good or a person educated? What is education for? In such a test, actors (including the interviewer) may agree or disagree about the relevant type of value to be brought to bear on a situation; if they agree on this, they may nonetheless disagree about the best way to assess such worth; when experiencing subjective disagreement, they may express it or choose to let the situation 'rub along', perhaps with an idea of picking one's battles; and throughout all this, they may slip between different value systems to explain their complex beliefs.

The following passage comes from my interview with Tim, a dean at a post-war institution. I am following up his casual assertion, discussed in Chapter 6, that there was an institutional drive for more privately educated students. Make of my subtlety what you will:

Kathryn: It's just – I don't want to dwell on this too much, but I was really interested when you said that there was a drive – presumably this is something that wasn't talked about publicly – but the idea that the university was particularly keen to have more private school students. I'm not sure if that's what you meant to say. For what reason? What was the thinking behind that?
Tim: High tariff.
Kathryn: Mmm. Okay. But was that –?
Tim: Remember – you see at the time, when we were talking about this kind of problem, the problem that we had was that the typical grades of the students who came to us were basically BBC. So, you're talking about, now you're talking about eight, nine years ago: BBC. Now you see that in the thrall of the league tables, and it's perfectly obvious that, you know, if you're attracting BBC – or possibly worse – then effectively you are gonna be much lower down in the league table. Now, to any vice chancellor who wants to improve the quality of his or her institution, then one of the ways you do that is by improving the quality of the students.

In the preceding encounter, in a manner appropriate to the polite and quasi-formal setting, I began to externalise a cognitive disagreement I was having with the participant. As discussed in Chapter 6, Tim was painting a complex picture of the liberal arts student, making appeals to both domestic and civic types of worth. Clearly, it was the appeal to the domestic and, in particular, what I took to be a suggestion that private school students may be equipped with a disposition particularly well suited to the liberal arts, that troubled me and that I wished to press. Indirectly, I questioned the justness of the wish to recruit more private school students: "What was the thinking behind that?" The composite situation, where very different sorts of value are blithely compounded, has produced a certain awkwardness, and I want to clear it up. This is a press for justification.

However, it would be too simplistic to say that Tim pulls the 'correct answer' out of his hat, at this moment, only when pressed: he was already appealing to high tariff in the less disputational earlier discussion. It was only when the interview began to be raised to the level of a dispute that specific ideas about justice were settled on, in the form of justifications: the desire for private school students does not have to do with a domestic preoccupation with a certain type of 'well-bred' student, but rather with a contextually appropriate set of civic and managerial concerns. We see such justifications as legitimating illusions only if we ignore the more complex, multi-register ways in which people speak at other times.

The interview is clearly a heightened and highly reflective encounter, and far from identical to the debates that emerge in the everyday business of trying to get a degree going and maintained. However, this is not to say that these reflections are at a complete remove from that reality either (de Nanteuil, 2021). The ambivalence, as well as the potential for conflict and justification, are heightened but not introduced by the interview; we might say that universities as everyday spaces are pregnant with conflicts between value systems. As I have tried to argue throughout, interviews will not unveil the fundamental truth of what people think, but this is not because they are artificial types of interaction. Rather, it is because they are interactions of a particular sort, encouraging some ways of speaking and not others. In this way, they are no different from any other type of encounter (Hughes et al, 2020). If we think of motivations, beliefs and value systems as plural, we need not scold interview techniques for their inability to get to the fundamental truth of the matter.

Sociologists' requests that interviewees show their working and explicitly reflect on what are normally practical acts of doing may not be everyday types of request, and they may cause people to pause, to stumble, to appear to become defensive or even to contradict themselves. However, it would be a mistake to take this to mean that people were not, in fact, in the habit of trying to make just decisions when in action.

As explained in the introduction to this book, people can be conceptualised as competent in justice just as they are competent in the grammar of their native tongue (Boltanski and Thévenot, 2000). Asked by a linguist to explain the rules, they may take some time to articulate them, but this does not mean that the idea of a grammatical system is new to them, nor that their speech until that point had consisted of a pre-reflective instinct. Language is a practice, true, but we make *conscious* attempts to do it better, and so we generally get more competent as we go along. People likewise think about the justness of their decisions and their beliefs as they go along (Sayer, 2011), even if, as a particular type of encounter, an interview might encourage them to reflect more – or perhaps just differently: 'people do not ordinarily seek to invent false pretexts after the fact so as to cover up some secret motive, the way one comes up with an alibi; rather, they seek to carry out their actions in such a way that these can withstand the test of justification' (Boltanski and Thévenot, 2006: 37).

It is important to stress here that this way of thinking about interviews should also encourage us to think of *interviewers* as holding plural values that may be more or less foregrounded at different times. Like anyone else, sociologists might also agree, disagree, hold their tongue or seek a compromise when discussing whether a particular value system is being thought through in an appropriate way, or indeed whether the value system, or systems, being applied are appropriate at all. In the preceding encounter, it is not just Tim who is grappling with the questions of character, ability, merit and elitism. The disentangling of compounded values is a process that happens *between myself and Tim*, as active participants in the encounter.

My line of questioning has encouraged some form of justification from him, but I am also implicated in the same complex entanglements as Tim. Discussions not only about what makes a good or a bad student, but also more prosaically about student recruitment and even league-table positions (whether 'believed in' or not, they do matter in the actually existing world), are hardly alien to critical sociologists of education. It is the character of the research interview that means that I am not explicitly debating these points myself at this moment (though, clearly enough, some of my beliefs are affecting the way the conversation is going). Nonetheless, I am implicated in just this conflict.

This embroilment is one reason that the approach foregrounding plurality outlined in this book need not lead to a mere relativism that stops at the *observation* of plurality. I have not tried to explain the entanglements from the outside, but rather to engage, in extended form, with debates that students and academics were *already* having about the appropriate amount of weight a particular value system ought to have in a particular context (Susen, 2014). This is not to unveil the fundamental truth of the situation ('When deans say they want students with a higher tariff, they really mean they want students from private schools'), but to question the legitimacy of the *link* between civic and domestic values here.

The tyranny of the educated

In this final section, I press in a more sustained way this question of the appropriateness of domestic values to particular types of educational context, as well as the vexed issue of meritocracy that this question throws up. Engaging with, and departing from, both left-wing critiques claiming that 'meritocracy' is a way of euphemising and legitimating privilege, and right-wing arguments for parity of esteem between vocational and non-vocational education, I argue that thinking in terms of a plurality of values can more effectively inform a progressive politics of education than either approach.[1] Rather than stopping at the mere observation of plurality – the relativism of which French pragmatic sociology is sometimes accused (Jensen, 2018) – such an argument contributes to the long history of criticism of meritocracy, though from a fundamentally different angle than the unveiling, or unmasking, style of critique (Baehr, 2019).

While meritocracy itself, as an ideology masking privilege, has often been critiqued from the Left (for recent examples, see Littler, 2018; Sandel, 2020), the use of non-vocational credentials to determine what is *meant* by merit has often (though by no means exclusively) been criticised from the Right. David Goodhart's (2020) *Head Hand Heart* is a recent case in point, arguing that caring and technical work should be regarded, and rewarded, as highly as those more intellectual forms of work associated with a university degree.

Arguing for parity of esteem, however, is not the same as suggesting how we might get there. To do that, we need to think about the specific mechanisms by which esteem comes to be distributed. To make the argument without examining the mechanisms (for instance, by claiming that 'too many' young people are going to university) will simply reinforce existing inequalities by limiting opportunities for the already disenfranchised. In the actually existing world, the claim that too many children have gone to university is more or less indistinguishable from the claim that, in Patrick Ainley's (2016a: 68, emphases added) words, 'too many of the *wrong sort* of children had gone to the *wrong sort* of universities'. The title of Paul Temple's (2020) instructive review of Goodhart's book points to the problem when those who have had the benefit of a non-vocational education and hope for the same for their own children seek to deny it to others: 'Why don't other people's children become plumbers?'

Saying that limiting university attendance *shouldn't* have regressive effects, and stopping there, is a bit like saying that if my nan had wheels she'd be a

---

[1] While the 'parity of esteem' argument can be made from both the Left and the Right (indeed, as an abstract idea, it's quite difficult to disagree with), in practical terms, it tends to come down to streaming for 'ability' and fewer university places.

bus. We need to think, in addition, about what it is about our society that means that fewer people going to university *is* a socially regressive idea, whether we like to think of ourselves as progressive or not. In particular, we need to understand something about inflation (Collins, 1979).

In the 20th century, credentialism (or society's prizing of civic values like educational qualifications) broke the elite's power, which had until then rested on birthright, or domestic considerations of nobility. Yet, it was precisely the *same* elite who attained the credentials necessary to succeed in this brave new world. In the next phase, this prizing of credentials led to massification: more and more of those who were able to do so sought to win by those means (an undergraduate degree) that seemed to mark out society's successes. It was – and is – a perfectly rational response, but it is taken in a broader context that is anything but rational. For once the elite realise that undergraduate degrees are no longer marking them out, then they're off: to postgraduate degrees, extra-curricular activities, prestigious and unpaid internships, or any other means they can find to distinguish themselves from the masses.

Chapter 6 of this book argued that there is a re-entanglement of domestic values into education in this inflationary situation, so that character is being tested for. Character is being tested for both in how liberal arts applicants are judged and in how attributes like individuality and single-mindedness are said to mark out the liberal arts graduate. Importantly, ideas about the ideal liberal arts student stress individual qualities with a decidedly classed bent: poise, well-roundedness, flair or polish. What we see in the re-entanglement of domestic values in education today is the emergence of some new criteria to allow pre-existing elites to continue to distinguish themselves.

While we may break the elite's monopoly on this or that *particular* good, then, such a break does not seem to affect their stranglehold on position, power, esteem or wealth. We are at an impasse. As Michael Walzer (1983: 18) notes:

> Simple equality is a simple distributive condition, so that if I have fourteen hats and you have fourteen hats, we are equal. And it is all to the good if hats are dominant, for then our equality is extended through all the spheres of social life. On the view that I shall take here, however, we simply have the same number of hats, and it is unlikely that hats will be dominant for long.

Contra a mantra of simple equality, if I have a degree and you have a degree, we are not equal. The next question is: how is such an absurd situation tolerated?

As we saw in Chapter 6, meritocracy (or at least in its post-war, 'fluid' form [Allen, 2014]) stresses aspiration and hard work, insisting that starting points should not determine end points. While Michael Young's (1958) originally satirical formulation of intelligence plus effort equals merit has remained central, it is the second part of the equation that has grown in stature. From the comprehensivisation movement on, aspiration and hard work have been our watchwords.

Aspiration, though, only makes sense when working hand in hand with desert. I go to university because I will then *deserve* goods that are not really educational concerns, and this allows multiple positive values to stick to individuals. In the credentialist era, when the elite monopolised higher education, civic values were dominant, and this meant not just that a degree opened doors to particular types of work, but that someone with a degree could expect to accrue more money, position, influence and respect. Our competitive and aspirational understanding of meritocracy assumes that this accrual is both inevitable and just, and the progressive educational beliefs that opened up higher education from the 1950s on likewise rested on this assumption of desert. In the current turn to character, we see similar processes unfold. Well-roundedness, flexibility and cosmopolitanism are prized not only for their intrinsic worth, but also because they mean other benefits are deserved – precisely those benefits that accrued to having a degree itself in the earlier period.

For aspiration to have any meaning, then, it requires hierarchy: I am aspiring to climb up and deserve more, not to fall down and deserve less. Parity of esteem remains an empty phrase because meritocracy relies on notions of better or worse options, better or worse outcomes, more or less worthy *people*. Without hierarchy, aspiration makes no sense, and this hierarchy is logically inconsistent with parity. In our actually existing society, 'moving up' means staying on longer in school, attending university and now attaining post-graduate qualifications too. This is why advocates of parity of esteem between vocational and non-vocational education still generally hope their own children will go to university.

As more people attend university, the differentiation better/worse simply rises up the chain, with better/worse university increasingly being used to distinguish between graduates. As Roger Brown (2018) has noted, the education system is quite singular in its capacity to create highly disparate outcomes (higher education institution attended, therefore job status, therefore money and power) on the basis of a difference between three As and three Bs at A level.

So more people going to university does not equalise anything, and yet fewer people going to university will be regressive. This seems contradictory, yet the reason that these apparently opposed solutions do not solve anything is that they rely on the same misidentification of the problem. Monopoly of one specific type of good by a small group is not the problem. The problem is not one of exclusion, but one of dominance: not that everyone cannot access the one type of good that determines the social hierarchy at the moment, but that there *is* one good that determines this at all.

Current attempts to universalise domestic worth (through character education in comprehensive schools, for instance) will, as before, merely move the competition somewhere else, and the currency of character will be worth no more than 'simply' having an undergraduate degree today. There have been countless attempts in recent years to make elitist conceptions of character and culture the centre of non-elite education, as in many Gove and post-Gove reforms to the national curriculum. Initiatives like this in fact have a lot in common with progressive attempts to broaden out from narrow, elitist notions of what terms like 'culture' and 'character' mean. In the end, they will have the same inflationary effects. These seemingly opposed currents in fact share the premise that is the problem: that attaining worth, credibility or value in one sphere ought to lead to benefits in another. Power, prestige, wealth and position do not accrue to pre-existing elites because they monopolise domestic worth (or, before that, civic worth); if they did, then moves to democratise access to, or common understandings of, these worths would succeed in smoothing out social hierarchies, rather than producing inflationary effects. Rather, it is the prizing of some particular type of good as superior to others that paradoxically moves the competitive struggle along to somewhere else.

The argument is not that a liberal arts education is not a good type of education. Rather, it is that it should not be used to sift 'better' from 'worse' students (as in some senior academics' invocations of student 'quality'), nor to insist on a denigration of either technical or specialist education. Liberal arts degrees end up being presented as a superior form of education (in both explicit and implicit ways) not because they mask class struggle under a veil of civic legitimacy, but because they entangle multiple forms of value (domestic, civic, inspirational, market) together in complex ways that allow different types of good (credentials, intellectual kudos, social esteem, future pay) to stick to individuals. Some students' and academics' attempts to disentangle these worths and make conscious decisions about what we mean to test for in educational spaces are a first step in winding back claims made elsewhere about the liberal arts' inherent superiority over other types of education. They are also a first step in making these spaces less elitist.

References

Adler, M.J. (1988) *Reforming Education: The Opening of the American Mind* (2nd edn), Basingstoke: Macmillan.

Ahmed, S. (2015) 'Against students', *New Inquiry*, 29 June. Available at: https://thenewinquiry.com/against-students/

Ainley, P. (2016a) *Betraying a Generation: How Education Is Failing Young People*, Bristol: Policy Press.

Ainley, P. (2016b) 'The Business Studies University: turning higher education into further education', *London Review of Education*, 14(1): 106–15.

Allen, A. (2014) *Benign Violence: Education in and beyond the Age of Reason*, New York: Palgrave Macmillan.

Allen, A. (2017) *The Cynical Educator*, Leicester: Mayfly.

Allen, K. and Bull, A. (2018) 'Following policy: a network ethnography of the UK character education policy community', *Sociological Research Online*, 23(2): 438–58.

Altbach, P.G. (2016) 'The many traditions of liberal arts – and their global relevance', *International Higher Education*, 84: 21–3.

Andersen, N. (2007) 'The self-infantilised adult and the management of personality', *Critical Discourse Studies*, 4(3): 331–52.

Arnold, M. (1993) *'Culture and Anarchy' and Other Writings*, Cambridge: Cambridge University Press.

Ashwin, P. (2020) *Transforming University Education: A Manifesto*, London: Bloomsbury.

Baehr, P. (2019) *The Unmasking Style in Social Theory*, Abingdon: Routledge.

Baker, J. (2012) 'How to get into the BBC as a journalist', *BBC College of Journalism*, 1 June. Available at: www.bbc.co.uk/blogs/collegeofjournalism/entries/7b45a1ec-e9fd-3f5d-9c0b-afe1051fe35a

Barrett, B.D. (2012) 'Is interdisciplinarity old news? A disciplined consideration of interdisciplinarity', *British Journal of Sociology of Education*, 33(1): 97–114.

Bartram, F. (2020) 'Barriers and facilitators in access to and progression within higher education: an exploration of first-generation students' experiences', BA dissertation, University of Sussex.

Basaure, M. (2011) 'An interview with Luc Boltanski: criticism and the expansion of knowledge', *European Journal of Social Theory*, 14(3): 361–81.

Bathmaker, A.-M., Ingram, N., Abrahams, J., Hoare, A., Waller, R. and Bradley, H. (2016) *Higher Education, Social Class and Social Mobility: The Degree Generation*, London: Palgrave Macmillan.

BBC Radio 4 (2017) 'More or less', 30 May. Available at: www.bbc.co.uk/programmes/p053ln9f

Bentham, J. (1983) *Constitutional Code Vol 1*, Oxford: Clarendon.

Berg, M. and Seeber, B.K. (2017) *The Slow Professor: Challenging the Culture of Speed in the Academy*, Toronto: University of Toronto Press.

Berlant, L. (2011) *Cruel Optimism*, Durham, NC: Duke University Press.

Bernstein, B. (1996) *Pedagogy, Symbolic Control and Identity: Theory, Research, Critique*, London: Taylor and Francis.

Bernstein, J.H. (2015) 'Transdisciplinarity: a review of its origins, development, and current issues', *Journal of Research Practice*, 11(1): 1–20.

Biesta, G. (2010) *Good Education in an Age of Measurement: Ethics, Politics, Democracy*, New York: Routledge.

Blatterer, H. (2007) 'Adulthood: the contemporary redefinition of a social category', *Sociological Research Online*, 12(4): 1–11.

Boltanski, L. (2011) *On Critique: A Sociology of Emancipation*, Cambridge: Polity.

Boltanski, L. and Thévenot, L. (1999) 'The sociology of critical capacity', *European Journal of Social Theory*, 2(3): 359–77.

Boltanski, L. and Thévenot, L. (2000) 'The reality of moral expectations: a sociology of situated judgement', *Philosophical Explorations*, 3(3): 208–31.

Boltanski, L. and Chiapello, E. (2005) *The New Spirit of Capitalism*, London: Verso.

Boltanski, L. and Thévenot, L. (2006) *On Justification: Economies of Worth*, Oxford: Princeton University Press.

Bourdieu, P. (1988) *Homo Academicus*, Cambridge: Polity.

Bourdieu, P. (1996) *The State Nobility: Elite Schools in the Field of Power*, Cambridge: Polity.

Bourdieu, P. and Passeron, J.-C. (1979) *The Inheritors: French Students and their Relation to Culture*, Chicago, IL: University of Chicago Press.

Boyle, M.-E. (2019) 'Global liberal education: theorizing emergence and variability', *Research in Comparative and International Education*, 14(2): 231–48.

Bradley, H. (2014) 'Class descriptors or class relations? Thoughts towards a critique of Savage et al', *Sociology*, 48(3): 429–36.

Brewer, D.J., Gates, S. and Goldman, C. (2002) *In Pursuit of Prestige: Strategy and Competition in US Higher Education*, Somerset, NJ: Transaction.

Brewer, T. (2018) 'What good are the humanities?', *Raritan*, 37(4): 98–118.

Brown, P. and Hesketh, A. (2004) *The Mismanagement of Talent: Employability and Jobs in the Knowledge Economy*, Oxford: Oxford University Press.

Brown, P., Hesketh, A. and Williams, S. (2003) 'Employability in a knowledge-driven economy', *Journal of Education and Work*, 16(2): 107–26.

Brown, P., Lauder, H. and Ashton, D. (2011) *The Global Auction: The Broken Promises of Education, Jobs, and Incomes*, Oxford: Oxford University Press.

Brown, P., Lauder, H. and Sung, J. (2015) 'Higher education, corporate talent and the stratification of knowledge work in the global labour market', in A. van Zanten, S.J. Ball and B. Darchy-Koechlin (eds) *World Yearbook of Education 2015. Elites, Privilege and Excellence: The National and Global Redefinition of Educational Advantage*, Abingdon: Routledge, pp 217–30.

Brown, R. (2018) 'Higher education and inequality', *Perspectives: Policy and Practice in Higher Education*, 22(2): 37–43.

Brown, W. (2006) *Regulating Aversion: Tolerance in the Age of Identity and Empire*, Oxford: Princeton University Press.

Brynin, M. (2012) 'Individual choice and risk: the case of higher education', *Sociology*, 47(2): 284–300.

Budd, R. (2018) 'Eliciting the institutional myth: exploring the ethos of "the university" in Germany and England', *European Journal of Higher Education*, 8(2): 135–51.

Burke, C. (2016) *Culture, Capitals and Graduate Futures: Degrees of Class*, London: Routledge.

Burke, P.J. and McManus, J. (2011) 'Art for a few: exclusions and misrecognitions in higher education admissions practices', *Discourse: Studies in the Cultural Politics of Education*, 32(5): 699–712.

Cantillon, B. and Van Lancker, W. (2013) 'Three shortcomings of the social investment perspective', *Social Policy and Society*, 12(4): 553–64.

Cassell, C. (2005) 'Creating the interviewer: identity work in the management research process', *Qualitative Research*, 5(2): 167–79.

Centre for Longitudinal Studies (2010) 'Millennium mothers want university education for their children', Centre for Longitudinal Studies, 15 October. Available at: https://cls.ucl.ac.uk/millennium-mothers-want-university-education-for-their-children/

Chandler, J. and Davidson, A.I. (2009) 'Introduction: doctrines, disciplines, discourses, departments', *Critical Inquiry*, 35(4): 729–46.

Claus, J., Meckel, T. and Pätz, F. (2018) 'The new spirit of capitalism in European liberal arts programs', *Educational Philosophy and Theory*, 50(11): 1011–19.

Collini, S. (1993) *Public Moralists: Political Thought and Intellectual Life in Britain 1850–1930*, Oxford: Oxford University Press.

Collini, S. (2012) *What Are Universities For?*, London: Penguin.

Collins, H. and Evans, R. (2007) *Rethinking Expertise*, London: University of Chicago Press.

Collins, R. (1979) *The Credential Society: An Historical Sociology of Education and Stratification*, New York: Academic Press.

Conley, J. (2015) 'Luc Boltanski and the cult of the individual theorist', *Canadian Journal of Sociology*, 40(3): 377–89.

De Nanteuil, M. (2021) *Justice in the Workplace: Overcoming Ethical Dilemmas*, Cheltenham: Edward Elgar.

Department for Business, Innovation and Skills (2016) *Success as a Knowledge Economy: Teaching Excellence, Social Mobility and Student Choice*, London: HMSO.

Department for Education (2015) 'Nicky Morgan launches rugby character drive with Saracens FC', Government Digital Service, 10 September. Available at: www.gov.uk/government/news/nicky-morgan-launches-rugby-character-drive-with-saracens-fc

Devos, A. (2003) 'Academic standards, internationalisation, and the discursive construction of "the international student"', *Higher Education Research and Development*, 22(2): 155–66.

Esping-Andersen, G. (2002) 'Towards the good society, once again?', in G. Esping-Anderson (ed) *Why We Need a New Welfare State*, Oxford: Oxford University Press, pp 1–25.

Esposito, E. (2015) 'Beyond the promise of security: uncertainty as resource', *Telos*, 170: 89–107.

European Commission (1995) *Teaching and Learning: Towards the Learning Society*, Brussels: European Commission.

European Commission (2008) *Improving Competences for the 21st Century: An Agenda for European Cooperation on Schools*, Brussels: European Commission.

Fassin, D. (2013) *Enforcing Order: An Ethnography of Urban Policing*, Cambridge: Polity.

Flexner, A. (2017) *The Usefulness of Useless Knowledge*, Princeton, NJ: Princeton University Press.

Friedman, S. and Laurison, D. (2019) *The Class Ceiling: Why It Pays to Be Privileged*, Bristol: Policy Press.

Frunzaru, V., Vătămănescu, E.-M., Gazzola, P. and Bolisani, E. (2018) 'Challenges to higher education in the knowledge economy: anti-intellectualism, materialism and employability', *Knowledge Management Research and Practice*, 16(3): 388–401.

Gaztambide-Fernández, R. (2011) 'Bullshit as resistance: justifying unearned privilege among students at an elite boarding school', *International Journal of Qualitative Studies in Education*, 24(5): 581–6.

Gibson-Graham, J.K. (2006) *The End of Capitalism (As We Knew It): A Feminist Critique of Political Economy* (2nd edn), London: University of Minnesota Press.

Giraud, E.H. (2019) *What Comes after Entanglement? Activism, Anthropocentrism, and an Ethics of Exclusion*, London: Duke University Press.

Godwin, K.A. (2015a) 'The counter narrative: critical analysis of liberal education in global context', *New Global Studies*, 9(3): 223–43.

Godwin, K.A. (2015b) 'The worldwide emergence of liberal education', *International Higher Education*, 79: 2–4.

Godwin, K.A. (2018) 'Legitimizing liberal arts and science institutions', *CIHE Perspectives*, 9: 12–14.

Godwin, K.A. and Pickus, N. (2017) *Liberal Arts and Sciences Innovation in China: Six Recommendations to Shape the Future*, Chestnut Hill, MA: Center for International Higher Education, Boston College.

Goodhart, D. (2020) *Head Hand Heart: The Struggle for Dignity and Status in the 21st Century*, London: Penguin.

Great Lakes Feminist Geography Collective (2015) 'For slow scholarship: a feminist politics of resistance through collective action in the neoliberal university', *ACME: An International E-Journal for Critical Geographies*, 14(4): 1235–59.

Hammersley, M. (2013) 'On the ethics of interviewing for discourse analysis', *Qualitative Research*, 14(5): 529–41.

Harding, S. (1991) *Whose Science? Whose Knowledge? Thinking from Women's Lives*, Milton Keynes: Open University Press.

Harpham, G.G. (2011) *The Humanities and the Dream of America*, Chicago, IL: University of Chicago Press.

Hartley, S. (2017) *The Fuzzy and the Techie: Why the Liberal Arts Will Rule the Digital World*, Boston, MA: Mariner.

Hartmann, M. (2007) *The Sociology of Elites*, Abingdon: Routledge.

Harward, D.W. (2018) *Liberal Education and We*, Warsaw: Artes Liberales Foundation.

Hemmings, C. (2005) 'Telling feminist stories', *Feminist Theory*, 6(2): 115–39.

Hogan, J. (2012) 'Restructuring revisited: changing academic structures in UK universities', *Perspectives: Policy and Practice in Higher Education*, 16(4): 129–35.

Holmqvist, D. (2022) 'A cry, a clash and a parting: a French pragmatic sociology approach to "the struggle over the teacher's soul"', *International Studies in Sociology of Education*, 31(3): 347–66.

Hughes, J., Hughes, K., Sykes, G. and Wright, K. (2020) 'Beyond performative talk: critical observations on the radical critique of reading interview data', *International Journal of Social Research Methodology*, 23(5): 547–63.

Hughson, T.A. and Wood, B.E. (2022) 'The OECD Learning Compass 2030 and the future of disciplinary learning: a Bernsteinian critique', *Journal of Education Policy*, 37(4): 634–54.

Hurst, A.L. (2013) 'Student types as reflection of class habitus: an application of Bourdieu's scholastic fallacy', *Theory and Research in Education*, 11(1): 43–61.

Ingram, N. and Allen, K. (2019) '"Talent-spotting" or "social magic"? Inequality, cultural sorting and constructions of the ideal graduate in elite professions', *Sociological Review*, 67(3): 723–40.

Institute for Government (2018) 'The civil service fast stream'. Available at: www.instituteforgovernment.org.uk/explainers/civil-service-fast-stream

James, D. (2015) 'How Bourdieu bites back: recognising misrecognition in education and educational research', *Cambridge Journal of Education*, 45(1): 97–112.

Jensen, J.D. (2018) 'Justice in reality: overcoming moral relativism in Luc Boltanski's pragmatic sociology of critique', *Distinktion: Journal of Social Theory*, 19(3): 268–85.

Jerome, L. and Kisby, B. (2019) *The Rise of Character Education in Britain: Heroes, Dragons and the Myths of Character*, London: Palgrave Macmillan.

Jones, H.S. (2007) *Intellect and Character in Victorian England: Mark Pattison and the Invention of the Don*, Cambridge: Cambridge University Press.

Jones, S. (2015) 'Nonacademic indicators and the higher education admissions process: a case study of the personal statement', in V. Stead (ed) *International Perspectives on Higher Education Admissions Policy: A Reader*, New York: Peter Lang, pp 291–99.

Kimball, B.A. (1986) *Orators and Philosophers: A History of the Idea of Liberal Education*, New York: Teachers' College Press.

Kontowski, D. (2016) 'The paradox of "practical liberal arts": lessons from the Wagner College case for liberal (arts) education in Eastern Europe', *Educational Studies Moscow*, 3: 80–109.

Lahire, B. (2011) *The Plural Actor*, Cambridge: Polity.

Lahire, B. (2015) 'The limits of the field: elements for a theory of the social differentiation of activities', in M. Hilgers and E. Mangez (eds) *Bourdieu's Theory of Social Fields: Concepts and Applications*, Abingdon: Routledge, pp 62–101.

Littler, J. (2018) *Against Meritocracy: Culture, Power and Myths of Mobility*, Abingdon: Routledge.

Luhmann, N. (1976) 'The future cannot begin: temporal structures in modern society', *Social Research*, 43(1): 130–52.

Luhmann, N. (1998) *Observations on Modernity*, Stanford, CA: Stanford University Press.

Luhmann, N. (2002) *Theories of Distinction: Redescribing the Descriptions of Modernity*, Redwood City, CA: Stanford University Press.

Lumley, S. (2020) 'Hair salon banned from advert for "happy" stylist because it's discriminatory', *Mirror*, 3 September. Available at: www.mirror.co.uk/news/uk-news/hair-salon-banned-advert-happy-22622435

Mangez, E. and Vanden Broeck, P. (2020) 'The history of the future and the shifting forms of education', *Educational Philosophy and Theory*, 52(6): 676–87.

Mangset, M. (2015) 'Contextually bound authoritative knowledge: a comparative study of British, French and Norwegian administrative elites' merit and skills', in A. van Zenten, S.J. Ball and B. Darchy-Koechlin (eds) *Elites, Privilege and Excellence: The National and Global Redefinition of Educational Advantage*, Abingdon: Routledge, pp 201–16.

Marks, R. (2014) 'Educational triage and ability-grouping in primary mathematics: a case-study of the impacts on low-attaining pupils', *Research in Mathematics Education*, 16(1): 38–53.

Marvell, R. (2021) 'Social inequalities and the journey to postgraduate taught study: narratives and navigations of first-generation students in England', PhD thesis, University of Sussex, UK.

McArthur, J. (2011) 'Reconsidering the social and economic purposes of higher education', *Higher Education Research and Development*, 30(6): 737–49.

Messer-Davidow, E. (2002) *Disciplining Feminism: From Social Activism to Academic Discourse*, London: Duke University Press.

Meyerhoff, E. and Noterman, E. (2019) 'Revolutionary scholarship by any speed necessary: slow or fast but for the end of this world', *ACME: An International Journal for Critical Geographies*, 18(1): 217–45.

Moore, R. (2011) 'Making the break: disciplines and interdisciplinarity', in F. Christie and K. Maton (eds) *Disciplinarity: Functional Linguistic and Sociological Perspectives*, London: Continuum, pp 87–105.

Morgan, N. (2017) *Taught Not Caught: Educating for 21st Century Character*, Melton: John Catt.

Nordensvärd, J. (2010) 'The consumer metaphor versus the citizen metaphor: different sets of roles for students', in M. Molesworth, R. Scullion and E. Nixon (eds) *The Marketisation of Higher Education: The Student as Consumer*, Abingdon: Routledge, pp 157–69.

Nussbaum, M. (2010) *Not for Profit: Why Democracy Needs the Humanities*, Princeton, NJ: Princeton University Press.

Oakley, F. (1992) *Community of Learning: The American College and the Liberal Arts Tradition*, New York: Oxford University Press.

Oldenhof, L., Postma, J. and Putters, K. (2013) 'On justification work: how compromising enables public managers to deal with conflicting values', *Public Administration Review*, 74(1): 52–63.

Organisation for Economic Co-operation and Development (2019) *OECD Learning Compass 2030: A Series of Concept Notes*, Paris: Organisation for Economic Co-operation and Development.

Peck, J. and Theodore, N. (2000) 'Beyond "employability"', *Cambridge Journal of Economics*, 24: 729–49.

Pépin, L. (2007) 'The history of EU cooperation in the field of education and training: how lifelong learning became a strategic objective', *European Journal of Education*, 42(1): 121–32.

Pettinger, L. (2019) *What's Wrong with Work?*, Bristol: Policy Press.

Rata, E. (2016) 'A pedagogy of conceptual progression and the case for academic knowledge', *British Educational Research Journal*, 42(1): 168–84.

Reay, D. and Ball, S.J. (1998) '"Making their minds up": family dynamics of school choice', *British Educational Research Journal*, 24(4): 431–48.

Resnik, J. (2012) 'The denationalization of education and the expansion of the international baccalaureate', *Comparative Education Review*, 56(2): 248–69.

Robbins, L., Anderson, D., Anderson, K., Chenevix-Trench, A., Drever, J., Elvin, H.L. et al (1963) *Higher Education: Report of the Committee Appointed by the Prime Minister under the Chairmanship of Lord Robbins*, London: HMSO.
Roitman, J. (2013) *Anti-Crisis*, Durham, NC: Duke University Press.
Rothblatt, S. (1976) *Tradition and Change in English Liberal Education: An Essay in History and Culture*, London: Faber and Faber.
Sandel, M. (2020) *The Tyranny of Merit: What's Become of the Common Good?*, London: Allen Lane.
Sardoč, M. and Deželan, T. (2021) 'Talents and distributive justice: some tensions', *Educational Philosophy and Theory*, 53(8): 768–76.
Savery, J.R. (2015) 'Overview of problem-based learning: definitions and distinctions', in A. Walker, H. Leary, C.E. Hmelo-Silver and P.A. Ertmer (eds) *Essential Readings in Problem-Based Learning: Exploring and Extending the Legacy of Howard S. Barrows*, West Lafayette, IN: Purdue University Press, pp 5–15.
Sayer, A. (1999) 'Bourdieu, Smith and disinterested judgement', *Sociological Review*, 47(3): 403–31.
Sayer, A. (2011) *Why Things Matter to People: Social Science, Values and Ethical Life*, Cambridge: Cambridge University Press.
Sayer, A. (2020) 'Critiquing – and rescuing – "character"', *Sociology*, 53(3): 460–81.
Schmitz, A., Flemmen M. and Rosenlund, L. (2018) 'Social class, symbolic domination, and *Angst*: the example of the Norwegian social space', *Sociological Review*, 66(3): 623–44.
Scott, P. (2002) 'The future of general education in mass higher education systems', *Higher Education Policy*, 15: 61–75.
Scott, P. (2012) 'Crossing boundaries: mass higher education in multiple perspectives', *Higher Education in Review*, 9: 1–14.
Scott, P. (2021) *Retreat or Resolution? Tackling the Crisis of Mass Higher Education*, Bristol: Policy Press.
Shattuck, R. (1973) 'Contract and credentials: the humanities in higher education', in C. Kaysen (ed) *Content and Context: Essays on College Education*, New York: McGraw Hill, pp 65–118.
Small, H. (2013) *The Value of the Humanities*, Oxford: Oxford University Press.
Smith, D. (1987) *The Everyday World as Problematic: A Feminist Sociology*, Boston, MA: Northeastern University Press.
Susen, S. (2014) 'Luc Boltanski: his life and work – an overview', in S. Susen and B.S. Turner (eds) *The Spirit of Luc Boltanski: Essays on the 'Pragmatic Sociology of Critique'*, London: Anthem, pp 3–28.
Swift, J. (1958) *A Tale of a Tub; to Which Is Added the Battle of the Books and Mechanical Operation of the Spirit*, London: Oxford University Press.
Telling, K. (2016) 'Bourdieu and the problem of reflexivity: recent answers to some old questions', *European Journal of Social Theory*, 19(1): 146–56.

Telling, K. (2018) 'Selling the liberal arts degree in England: unique students, generic skills and mass higher education', *Sociology*, 52(6): 1290–306.

Telling, K. (2019) 'Different universities, different temporalities: placing the acceleration of academic life in context', *Perspectives: Policy and Practice in Higher Education*, 23(4): 132–7.

Telling, K. (2020) 'The complexity of educational elitism: moving beyond misrecognition', *British Journal of Sociology of Education*, 41(7): 927–41.

Telling, K. and Serapioni, M. (2019) 'The rise and change of the competence strategy: reflections on twenty-five years of skills policies in the EU', *European Educational Research Journal*, 18(4): 387–406.

Temple, P. (2020) 'Why don't other people's children become plumbers?', *SRHE blog*, 19 October. Available at: https://srheblog.com/2020/10/19/why-dont-other-peoples-children-become-plumbers/

Thévenot, L. (2014) 'Enlarging conceptions of testing moments and critical theory: *Economies of Worth*, *On Critique*, and *Sociology of Engagements*', in S. Susen and B.S. Turner (eds) *The Spirit of Luc Boltanski: Essays on the 'Pragmatic Sociology of Critique'*, London: Anthem, pp 245–61.

Tholen, G. (2014) *The Changing Nature of the Graduate Labour Market: Media, Policy and Political Discourses in the UK*, Basingstoke: Palgrave Macmillan.

Tholen, G. (2017) 'Symbolic closure: towards a renewed sociological perspective on the relationship between higher education, credentials and the graduate labour market', *Sociology*, 51(5): 1067–83.

Tholen, G., James Relly, S., Warhurst, C. and Commander, J. (2016) 'Higher education, graduate skills and the skills of graduates: the case of graduates as residential sales estate agents', *British Educational Research Journal*, 42(3): 508–23.

Tomlinson, M. (2008) '"The degree is not enough": students' perceptions of the role of higher education credentials for graduate work and employability', *British Journal of Sociology of Education*, 29(1): 49–61.

Turner, R.H. (1960) 'Sponsored and contest mobility and the school system', *American Sociological Review*, 25(6): 855–67.

Van der Wende, M. (2017) 'The emergence of liberal arts and sciences education in Europe: a comparative perspective', in P. Marber and D. Araya (eds) *The Evolution of Liberal Arts in the Global Age*, New York: Routledge, pp 106–26.

Vora, N. (2019) *Teach for Arabia: American Universities, Liberalism, and Transnational Qatar*, Stanford, CA: Stanford University Press.

Vostal, F. (2016) *Accelerating Academia: The Changing Structure of Academic Time*, Basingstoke: Palgrave Macmillan.

Walzer, M. (1983) *Spheres of Justice: A Defense of Pluralism and Equality*, New York: Basic.

Warrell, H. (2015) 'UK private university trains guests at "dinner of life"', *Financial Times*, 12 June. Available at: www.ft.com/content/28e10312-1102-11e5-8413-00144feabdc0

Weenink, D. (2008) 'Cosmopolitanism as a form of capital: parents preparing their children for a globalizing world', *Sociology*, 42(6): 1089–106.

Wheelahan, L. (2007) 'How competency-based training locks the working class out of powerful knowledge: a modified Bernsteinian analysis', *British Journal of Sociology of Education*, 28(5): 637–51.

Williams, G. (2020) 'Management millennialism: designing the new generation of employee', *Work, Employment and Society*, 34(3): 371–87.

Williams, J. (2012) *Consuming Higher Education: Why Learning Can't Be Bought*, London: Bloomsbury.

Ye, R. and Nylander, E. (2021) 'Deservedness, humbleness and chance: conceptualisations of luck and academic success among Singaporean elite students', *International Studies in Sociology of Education*, 30(4): 401–21.

Young, M. (1958) *The Rise of the Meritocracy, 1870–2033: An Essay on Education and Equality*, London: Thames and Hudson.

Young, M.F.D. (2008) *Bringing Knowledge Back In: From Social Constructivism to Social Realism in the Sociology of Education*, Abingdon: Routledge.

Zakaria, F. (2015) *In Defense of a Liberal Education*, New York: Norton.

Index

References to footnotes show both the page number and the note number (39n3).

A

A levels 41–2, 43, 55
'abolitionist university studies' 1
abstract modules 45
academic acceleration 22
Adams, D. 27
adaptability 4, 23, 57–8, 74, 81, 89
admissions interviews 2, 127
admissions processes 125, 126
adulthood 64, 85–6, 105
Ahmed, S. 68, 108
Ainley, P. 21, 37, 76, 83, 111, 116, 141
Allen, A. 29, 58, 87, 94, 126, 127, 131, 142
Allen, K. 113, 118
Altbach, P. 6
ambitiousness 65, 67–8, 70, 96, 117
ambivalence, hierarchy of 7–11, 90, 137
analytical skills 79, 84, 118
Andersen, N.A. 60, 86
anxiety 85–9
applied learning 44–52
aristocratic undertones of liberal arts 20
  see also elites
Arnold, M. 55
artes liberales 23, 26–7
Ashwin, P. 60
aspiration 78, 84, 110, 113, 132, 142–3
assessments 47, 59, 77–8, 111, 116–17, 121, 126–8
autonomous learning 44, 54, 105

B

Baehr, P. 141
Baker, J. 118
Ball, S.J. 115
Barrett, B.D. 49, 62
Bartram, F. 95
Bathmaker, A.-M. 44, 123
Bentham, J. 127
Bernstein, J.H. 34, 45, 76, 115
bespoke degrees 65, 67
Biesta, G. 54
Blatterer, H. 64, 86, 87
Boltanski, L. 11, 12, 13, 14, 15, 18, 23, 28, 29, 54, 59, 69, 78, 81, 100, 106, 109, 111, 116, 119, 126, 132, 135, 137, 139, 140
Bourdieu, P. 3, 5, 71, 72, 116, 129, 132
Boyle, M-E. 4, 55, 134
Bradley, H. 10
breadth of subjects 41–2, 49–50, 55, 110

Brewer, D.J. 23, 50
Brown, P. 72, 83, 84, 89, 117, 118
Brown, R. 143
Brown, W. 99
Brynin, M. 85, 89
Budd, R. 108
Bull, A. 113
Burke, C. 72, 87
Burke, P.J. 54, 89
business case for liberal arts 20

C

Cantillon, B. 58
careerism 62, 75, 76
Cassell, C. 94
categories of institution 7
Chandler, J. 40
character
  and competences 57
  as 'domestic values' 2
  elitist notions of 115–21, 144
  entanglement with civic values 115–21, 142
  fairness 126–9
  'ideal' student identities 112, 113–15
  increases in character education 111–12, 126–9
  recruitment processes 2, 18, 115–21, 142
  testing for character 116–21
  see also domestic values
Chiapello, E. 14, 54, 100, 135
choice
  consumerism 102–8
  definition of 'liberal' 5
  employers' 77
  freedom of 124
  freedom to make bad 106
  individualist education 50–1, 77
  liberal arts delays need for 36, 85, 86
  parenting styles 114–15
  tensions of choice and progression 35–8
citizenship 90, 91–6
civic values
  common/public good 13, 92–3
  credentialism 142, 143
  definition 2
  knotted with domestic/individualist 92–3, 111, 115–21, 129, 139
Civil Service Fast Stream 84, 118
class *see* social class
Claus, J. 58, 89, 100
closure of degree programmes 27–9

155

cohort identity 121–2
collaborative working 59
  see also teamwork skills
collectivism 45
Collini, S. 46, 113
Collins, H. 47
Collins, R. 116, 142
combined honours (statistics on) 74
common core of general education 42
communality 96
communication skills 54, 58, 59, 93, 97
communities of learning 121–3, 124, 132
competences 57–60, 65
complex problems 46–8
  see also wicked problems
compulsory modules 49–50
  see also core modules
Conley, J. 15
Conservative governments 14
consumerism
  consumer rights narrative 107–8
  consumer students 90, 91, 102–8
  market value of degrees 32
  and notions of specialness 69
  universities' trend towards 4
  'what students want' 55
contact hours 39, 44, 105, 106, 107
context-dependent learning 32
core modules 32, 37, 44–52, 62, 70, 106
cosmopolitanisation 97
cosmopolitanism 90, 91, 96–102, 120, 143
cost effectiveness 20
  see also consumerism; marketisation of education
credentialism 142, 143
critical sociology of education 3, 12–13, 134, 140
critical thinking 23, 27, 45, 55
'critical university studies' 1
cynicism 10, 11, 94, 136

D

Davidson, A.I. 40
de Nanteuil, M. 139
debt 105
  see also tuition fees
deferred gratification 50–1
definition of 'liberal' 124
definition of 'liberal arts' 79–80, 124, 136
definitions of 'liberal' 5, 23
degree coherence 62
delayed choices, liberal arts allowing for 36, 85, 86
democratic values 93, 126
departments, academic 33, 39–40, 42–3
depersonalisation 111, 126, 127, 128
depth versus breadth 49–50
designing liberal arts courses 25–6
Devos, A. 101

Deželan, T. 131
dilettantes 129
'direction of travel' 22, 24–9
disciplines, academic 31–53, 60–1, 103
discontinuing liberal arts degrees 27–9
discourse analysis 7
domestic values
  critical sociology of education 12–13
  definition 2
  and elitism 72, 124, 139, 142, 144
  entanglement in liberal arts 18, 55
  and fairness 109, 126–9
  generalist, elite English education 72
  meritocracy and mass higher education 110–33
  see also character
dual-honours 36, 39

E

educational intimacy 112, 121–6, 129
educational tests 111, 112
  see also assessments
efficiencies 20
egalitarianism 8
elective modules 39, 40
elites
  access to jobs 83
  aristocratic undertones of liberal arts 20
  character 144
  cosmopolitanism 100
  credentialism 142
  desirable personal attributes 118
  'direction of travel' 25
  extra-curricular pursuits 71, 72
  'high-quality' student 120–1
  'ideal' student identities 119–20
  international elite versus home students 91
  massification 110
  meritocracy 143
  as narrative 1
  pace of change 29
  politics, philosophy and economics (PPE) 55, 64, 114
  prestige 67
  prestigious universities, value of 8, 23
  recruitment processes 117
  social justice 93, 95
  symbolic closure 116
  see also Oxbridge
employability
  applied learning 50
  choice of degree 118
  consumer students 103–4
  cosmopolitanism 97
  degree classification 61
  generic skills and the unique student 54, 55–6, 57
  versus intrinsic worth of education 14

Index

market value of degrees 13, 54–7
massification 116
and non-vocational degrees 74–89
skills and competences 57–60
standing out 69–72
entry-level modules (101) 39, 42, 43
epistemology 45
Esping-Anderson, G. 58
Esposito, E. 82
ethnicity 9, 68, 90, 101
European Commission 54, 58, 92
European tradition of liberal education 26–7
Evans, R. 47
exam hounds 129
exams 126–7
see also assessments
expertise, development of 48–50, 55, 60–4, 65
extra-curricular pursuits 70–2, 117

F

fairness 3, 109, 112, 121, 126–9
Fassin, D. 136
feedback 103
field (Bourdieu) 5
financial safety nets 86, 87, 89
first-generation students 14, 83, 85–6, 91, 96, 100, 114–15, 137
Flexner, A. 47
freedom, literal 23, 124
Friedman, S. 118
Frunzaru, V. 102
Further and Higher Education Act 1992 7
future, unknowability of the 21, 63, 75, 81–4

G

Gaztambide-Fernández, R. 130–1
gender 69, 101
General Studies (A level) 55
generalism 55, 72, 77, 136
generic skills 54–73
Gibson-Graham, J.K. 135
Giraud, E.H. 3, 109
global citizenship 92, 97, 100, 122
global liberal education 55
Godwin, K. 3–4, 6, 74
good citizens 90, 91–6
Goodhart, D. 141
'Googliness' 118
Gove, M. 144
Grayling, A. 55, 62
grit 111, 112, 113, 131

H

Hammersley, M. 137
happiness 17–18
hard work/effort 112–13, 129, 131

Harding, S. 8
Harpham, G.G. 99
Hartley, S. 10, 31
Hartmann, M. 132
Hemmings, C. 21
heritage 23
Hesketh, A. 72, 89, 117, 118
hierarchy of ambivalence 7–11, 90, 137
Higher Education Classification of Subjects 74
'high-quality' student 120, 126, 130, 132
history of the liberal arts 21, 23
Hogan, J. 39
holism 33, 36, 58
Holmqvist, D. 77
Hughes, J. 10, 94, 108, 139
Hughson, T.A. 46
Hurst, A.L. 62, 75
hyper-interdisciplinarity 31, 33, 45, 47, 51, 52, 76

I

'ideal' student identities 67–8, 90–109, 112, 116, 119–20, 126, 129, 142
idealism 10, 11, 75, 94
identity
  cohort identity 65
  and the 'ideal' student 90–109
  'real-world' learning 46
  relational 9
independence 114, 115, 118
individual flourishing 14
individualism
  civic values 93
  consumer students 102–8
  in the definition of liberal arts 4
  educational intimacy 121
  and intelligence/polymathy 68
  interdisciplinarity 45, 48–9, 50
  pursuit of personal interests 45
  social justice 95
  tensions of choice and progression 35–6, 38
  unique student 65–9
induction 122
industrial values
  aligned with marketisation of education 72, 75
  and employability 13, 54, 60, 77, 78, 79
  students' opinions of 59–60, 75, 88
  tensions of choice and progression 37
inequality
  extra-curricular pursuits 71
  historic 24
  individualisation of problems 113
  international students 9, 96
  massification 116, 141
  privilege 9, 10, 132, 141, 142–3
  structural educational inequalities 29, 84, 134

infrastructural constraints 38–44
Ingram, N. 58, 118
innovation 21–4, 25, 65
inspiration 27–8
instrumentalism 47–8, 55, 60, 68, 76, 97, 102, 104
intellectual rigour 78
intelligence 66–7, 68, 129–32, 143
intercultural sensitivity skills 58
interdisciplinarity 31–52, 61, 62, 93, 95
  see also hyper-interdisciplinarity; trans-disciplinarity
international baccalaureate (IB) 41, 43–4, 99, 119, 120, 123
international students 8–9, 22–3, 24, 96, 101
internships 70, 80, 82, 118
interpersonal relationships 111, 112, 116, 117–18
interview methods 7–11

J

James, D. 136
Jefferson, T. 130
Jensen, J.D. 85, 111, 141
jobs for life 86, 87
joint-honours 39, 45
Jones, H.S. 127
justice, competence in 8, 91–6, 139–40

K

Kimball, B. 50, 77, 127, 136
knowledge
  disciplines 34
  generalism 55
  importance of basic research 47
  skills and competences 57–60
  'true' 46
  unknowability of the future 21, 63, 75, 81–4
knowledge economy 57, 83
Kontowski, D. 6

L

Lahire, B. 5, 136
languages 40, 43, 49, 79, 96, 97
lateral thinking 54, 74
Laurison, D. 118
leadership, preparation for 93, 97, 114
league tables 110, 125, 140
learner-centred approaches 54
learnification 54, 55
learning outcomes 47, 76
lecturers 66, 78, 88, 108, 128
leftist politics 5, 91, 94, 95, 141
Lego analogy 37
liberal, definitions of 5, 23, 124
'liberal arts,' definition of 79–80, 124, 136

liberalism 99, 136
  see also neoliberalism
lifelong learners 58
low student numbers 28
Luhmann, N. 22, 81
Lumley, S. 17

M

majors 80
Mangez, E. 27, 76
Mangset, M. 55
market value of degrees
  employability 69–70, 75
  individual choice 35, 52–3, 61
  and notions of specialness 69
  prestige 24
  student recruitment 28
  teamwork skills 59
  see also employability
marketisation of education
  broader context of 4, 20
  civic values 13
  individualist general education 50
  modularisation 37
  as narrative 1
  scales of 135
  student recruitment 124
Marks, R. 66
Marvell, R. 63
massification 63–4, 69, 110–33, 142
master's programmes 63, 116
  see also postgraduate education
Maynard Hutchins, R. 93
McArthur, J. 59
McManus, J. 54, 89
McMaster medical school 45, 47
meritocracy 87, 110–33, 141–3
Messer-Davidow, E. 39
Meyerhoff, E. 126
mindfulness 88, 89
mobility 91, 99, 102
'modern liberal arts' 23–4
modularisation 37, 39
modules
  abstract modules 45
  compulsory modules 49–50
  core modules 32, 37, 44–52, 62, 70, 106
  elective modules 39, 40
  entry-level modules (101) 39, 42, 43
  prerequisite modules 37, 39, 107
Moore, R. 31, 33, 45
morality 58, 61–2, 66, 91, 93, 98, 130
Morgan, N. 113
multidisciplinarity 32, 33, 35, 36, 40, 45

N

name of 'liberal arts' 79–80
nationality 7, 68, 90, 101

Index

neoliberalism 5, 14, 135
networking 70, 122
New College of the Humanities 55
Newman, J.H. 127
Nordensvärd, J. 104
normative orders 11–12
nostalgia 1, 126
Noterman, E. 126
numbers, students as 126–7
numeracy 77, 79
Nussbaum, M. 92
Nylander, E. 132

O

Oakley, F. 121
OECD (Organisation for Economic Co-operation and Development) 46, 81
Oldenhof, L. 11, 135
Open University 74
open-mindedness 55–6, 65, 68, 91, 94, 96–102, 120
optionality, levels of 26
  see also choice
oral presentations 126, 127
Oxbridge 2, 84, 101, 122, 137

P

pace of change 27–9
parenting styles 114
parity of esteem 141, 143
parochialism 98–102
Passeron, J.-C. 116, 129
pathways, design of 6, 26, 80, 106
Pattison, M. 127
Pépin, L. 57
perseverance 114, 131
  see also grit; resilience
personalised learning 121, 126, 127–8
personality 111
  see also character
Pettinger, L. 5
philosophy, politics and economics (PPE) 55, 64, 114
Picasso, P. 11–12
pick-and-mix narratives 35–8, 77
polymathy 67, 68, 95, 112, 119, 120, 129, 130, 132
portfolio careers 84, 86, 89
positivism 34
post-disciplinary approaches 46
postgraduate education 41, 63, 143
power 8, 48, 90, 142, 143, 144
premium product 124–5
prerequisite modules 37, 39, 107
prestige
  age of English institutions 7
  elites 67
  knot of prestige and innovation 22–4
  market value of degrees 24
  prestigious universities, value of 23, 24
  progressiveness 144
  see also domestic values; elites
private education/privately-educated students
  Civil Service Fast Stream 84
  consumerism 105
  'high-quality' student 99, 119–20
  international baccalaureate (IB) 44, 99, 120
  polymathy and intelligence 68
  preparation for prestigious universities 101, 120
  privilege 9
  trying to attract 123, 124, 138–9
private institutions 87, 112
private sector jobs 61
privilege
  career planning 87
  cosmopolitanism 100
  exam systems 116
  extra-curricular pursuits 71
  individualism 65
  inequality 9, 10, 132, 141, 142–3
  meritocracy 141
  parenting styles 114–15
  private education 9
  UK over international students 101
problem-based learning 44–52
progression 37–8, 39, 41–4, 62
progressive mentalities 96, 98, 127, 141, 142, 143
project of the self 58, 92
promotional websites, as research source 7–8
psychometric tests 118
public service values 92, 94, 95
purposes of education 11, 14, 22, 60, 136, 138

Q

'quirkiness' 54

R

rankings 125
  see also league tables
rapid change 29
Rata, E. 32, 51
'real-world' learning 32, 34, 45–52, 55, 60, 75, 76–9
Reay, D. 115
reinvention, constant 28
Research Excellence Framework 40
research interviews, plurality in 137–40
research methods 7–11
research teams 45, 48
resilience 57, 58, 111, 112, 113, 114, 130
Resnik, J. 44
re-traditionalisation 20–1
right-wing politics 113, 141
rigour 62

risk, attitudes to 85, 86
Robbins Report 7
Roitman, J. 88
Rothblatt, S. 72, 113

S

Sardoč, M. 131
Savery, J.R. 45
Sayer, A. 11, 18, 104, 119, 139
Schmitz, A. 85
school qualifications 41, 63–4
  see also A levels; international baccalaureate (IB)
school-university transition 63–4
sciences
  A levels 42
  definition of 'liberal arts' 26
  employability 77
  interdisciplinarity 6, 34, 79
  specialisation 63
  US liberal arts courses 42
Scott, P. 110
self-assuredness 112, 113
self-directedness 114
Serapioni, M. 58
Shattuck, R. 48
sixth form study 41
  see also A levels; international baccalaureate (IB)
skills and competences 57–60, 65
slavery 23
slow scholarship movement 28
Small, H. 5
small class sizes 122, 123, 124
small cohorts 20, 112, 121, 132
Smith, D. 8
social capital 14
social class
  character 112, 113
  cosmopolitanism 96, 100, 101–2
  domestic values 55
  and the liberal arts 9
  masking class struggle 144
  mobility 99
  privately-educated students 68
  student identity 9, 65, 90
  'workingmiddle' class 83
  see also elites
social justice 8, 88, 90, 91–6
socio-economic backgrounds 9
Socratic teaching method 92
specialisation 39, 41–4, 55–73, 82, 119, 129
'standard adulthood' 64
standpoint theory 8
state-educated students 9, 88, 101, 112, 129
structured curriculum 62
  see also progression

student recruitment 20, 25, 28, 69, 110, 117, 124–5, 140
student satisfaction 102
student testimonials 66, 68–9, 71, 88, 102–3
student-staff ratios 110
  see also small class sizes
study abroad 99–100
style, personal 55, 110, 112, 116, 117
style, workplace 118–19
Susen, S. 140
Swift, J. 119

T

talent 67, 87–8, 129, 131–2
teaching quality 123
teamwork skills 54, 59, 114
technical expertise 48–9
Temple, P. 141
Thévenot, L. 11–12, 13, 18, 28, 59, 69, 78, 81, 106, 109, 111, 116, 119, 126, 132, 137, 139, 140
Tholen, G. 83, 116
timetabling 39, 107
T-levels 134
Tomlinson, M. 69
tradition 21, 22, 23, 24
trans-disciplinarity 34, 45, 48
transition to university 63–4
transversal competences 58, 59, 60
trendiness 25
tuition fees 104, 105, 107, 108, 125
Turner, R.H. 130
tutors 122–3, 128

U

unconscious bias training 2
unique student 65–9
US
  character education 113
  citizenship 92
  communities of learning 121
  departments and degrees 40
  differences from England 38–44
  disciplines 32
  English degrees marketed to 104
  influences in liberal arts tradition 137
  interdisciplinarity 42
  liberal arts 3, 5–6, 21, 26, 29, 36
  massification 63
  modularisation 37
  specialisation 41

V

van der Wende, M. 63
Van Lancker, W. 58
Vanden Broeck, P. 27, 76

vocational education 4, 6, 22, 27, 41, 55, 134, 143
Vora, N. 99
Vostal, F. 22
VUCA (volatile, uncertain, complex and ambiguous) future 81

W

Walzer, M. 127, 142
Warrell, H. 55
Weenink, D. 97
well-roundedness 96, 98, 102, 111, 113, 117, 142, 143
Western education and the liberal arts 6
Wheelahan, L. 33

wicked problems 31, 39n3, 46–9
widening participation 23–4, 74
Williams, G. 118
Williams, J. 102
Wood, B.E. 46
'workingmiddle' class 83

Y

Ye, R. 132
Young, M. 34, 55, 72, 113, 129, 131, 143
you-said-we-did mentality 103, 107

Z

Zakaria, F. 130